The Fighting Texas Navy
1832-1843

Douglas V. Meed

Republic of Texas Press
Plano, Texas

Library of Congress Cataloging-in-Publication Data

Meed, Douglas V.
 The fighting Texas Navy, 1832-1843. / Douglas V. Meed.
   p. cm.
 Includes bibliographical references (p.) and index.
 ISBN 1-55622-885-6 (pbk.)
 1. Texas--History, Naval--19th century. 2. Texas. Navy--History.
 3. Texas--History--Republic, 1836-1846. 4. Texas--History--
 Revolution, 1835-1836--Naval operations. I. Title.

 F390 .M528   2001
 976.4'04--dc21   2001031643
                                                                   CIP

© 2001, Douglas V. Meed
All Rights Reserved

Republic of Texas Press is an imprint of Wordware Publishing, Inc.
No part of this book may be reproduced in any form or by
any means without permission in writing from
Wordware Publishing, Inc.

Printed in the United States of America

ISBN 1-55622-885-6
10 9 8 7 6 5 4 3 2 1
0106

All inquiries for volume purchases of this book should be addressed to Wordware Publishing, Inc., at 2320 Los Rios Boulevard, Plano, Texas 75074. Telephone inquiries may be made by calling:

(972) 423-0090

To Robert Stonedale for his editing skills, nautical knowledge, research abilities, constant encouragement, and for his friendship of more than thirty-five years.

Thanks to Jeannine, Michael, Sonia, Geoffrey, and Alex for their help and encouragement.

Also thanks to the librarians at the Texas State Library, Austin; Center for American History, University of Texas at Austin; Austin Public Library; and the Rosenberg Library, Galveston.

Contents

List of Illustrations vi
Preface vii
Chapter 1—Opening Guns at Anahuac 1
Chapter 2—Clashes at Sea 19
Chapter 3—Of Pirates and Privateers. 36
Chapter 4—Successes and a Failure 61
Chapter 5—Sweeping the Mexican Main. 81
Chapter 6—Charging Lancers and a Castle. 92
Chapter 7—The New Navy and Old Troubles 106
Chapter 8—Scurvy, Storms, and a Silver Ransom 122
Chapter 9—Yucatan and a Mutiny 140
Chapter 10—Invasion, Betrayal, and a Duel 155
Chapter 11—A New Monster Threatens. 173
Chapter 12—Battle at Sea. 191
Chapter 13—The Decisive Battle 204
Chapter 14—Valor Betrayed. 215
L'Envoi 228
Bibliography. 231
Glossary 237
Index 241

List of Illustrations

Map of Campeche Campaign, 1843 2
George Fisher 5
Robert McAlpin "Three-Legged Willie" Williamson 15
"The Settlement of Austin's Colony" 20
Galveston in 1839 28-29
William Barret Travis 46
Schooner the *Brutus* 51
Antonio Lopez de Santa Anna 56
General Vicente Filisola 57
Schooner the *Independence* 76
William H. Wharton 79
Samuel Rhoads Fisher 87
Mirabeau Buonaparte Lamar 111
Texas sloop of war *Austin* 112
Commodore Moore's squadron 113
"Texas Navy Recruit" 119
Texas Schooner *San Antonio* 154
Texas Navy's steamship *Zavala* 171
Sam Houston 185
Brig the *Wharton* 219
Commodore Edwin Ward Moore 229

Preface

Brigadier General Theodore Roosevelt Jr. expressed it best when he wrote, "It is no exaggeration to say that without [the Texas navy] there would probably have been no Lone Star Republic and possibly the state of Texas would still be a part of Mexico."

During the violent years of the Texas Republic, its battered ships fought gallantly against the warships of Mexico while battling the raging storms and treacherous shoals of the Gulf of Mexico.

For a decade they dominated the third coast of North America, the Gulf of Mexico, from New Orleans to the Yucatan. Their control of these Gulf waters was critical to the very existence of the struggling republic.

The Texans did it with mostly cast-off ships and crews composed of both patriots and the scum of a hundred waterfronts. Throughout their ordeals they suffered from a government that had little appreciation of their sacrifices and at one time, labeled them common pirates.

Indeed, many of the navy's most difficult battles were waged against their sometimes president, Sam Houston.

Whether from personal pique, parsimonious attitude, or a failure to understand naval strategy, Houston did his best to scuttle the navy. Not content to rid Texas of its fighting ships, he also made Herculean efforts to destroy the men who sailed them. During Houston's bitter feuds, as vicious as any sea battles, he heaped lies, false charges, and ridicule on men who most Texans regarded as heroes.

Preface

    Had those men not had the moral courage to oppose their president as well as the physical courage to face Mexican gunfire, the independence of the new and fragile Republic of Texas would have been doomed.

    Sadly, most Americans, and for that matter most Texans, are unaware that Texas ever had a navy. While songs, poetry, folklore, and histories have made legendary the heroes of the Alamo, Goliad, and San Jacinto, the tough, enduring sailors of the Lone Star navy have been shrouded in obscurity.

    This is the heroic story of those seaborne Texans who were often outnumbered, usually outgunned, but never out-sailed and never, never outfought.

Chapter 1

Opening Guns at Anahuac

By the summer of 1832, tempers among the American settlers in the Galveston Bay area were heating up faster than the temperatures along the humid Gulf Coast. Whatever loyalty they felt for the government in Mexico City was fast evaporating.

It was never a love fest between the *Norte Americanos* and the Spaniards who first encouraged them to immigrate into Texas. And when the proud dons were driven out of Mexico during the revolution of 1824, the new government didn't become any more affectionate. But for a short while, it was in the interest of both parties to "just get along."

The Americans first settled in Texas during the 1820s when the Spanish and, for a few years, the Mexican governments awarded large grants of fertile land to immigrants who would settle north of the Rio Grande into the vast, almost empty lands called Tejas.

Both governments expected that the settlers would form a barrier against the Comanche, Kiowa, Apache, and other nomadic tribes whose raids had smashed the Spanish mission settlements in Texas. By the 1820s these raids had

Chapter 1

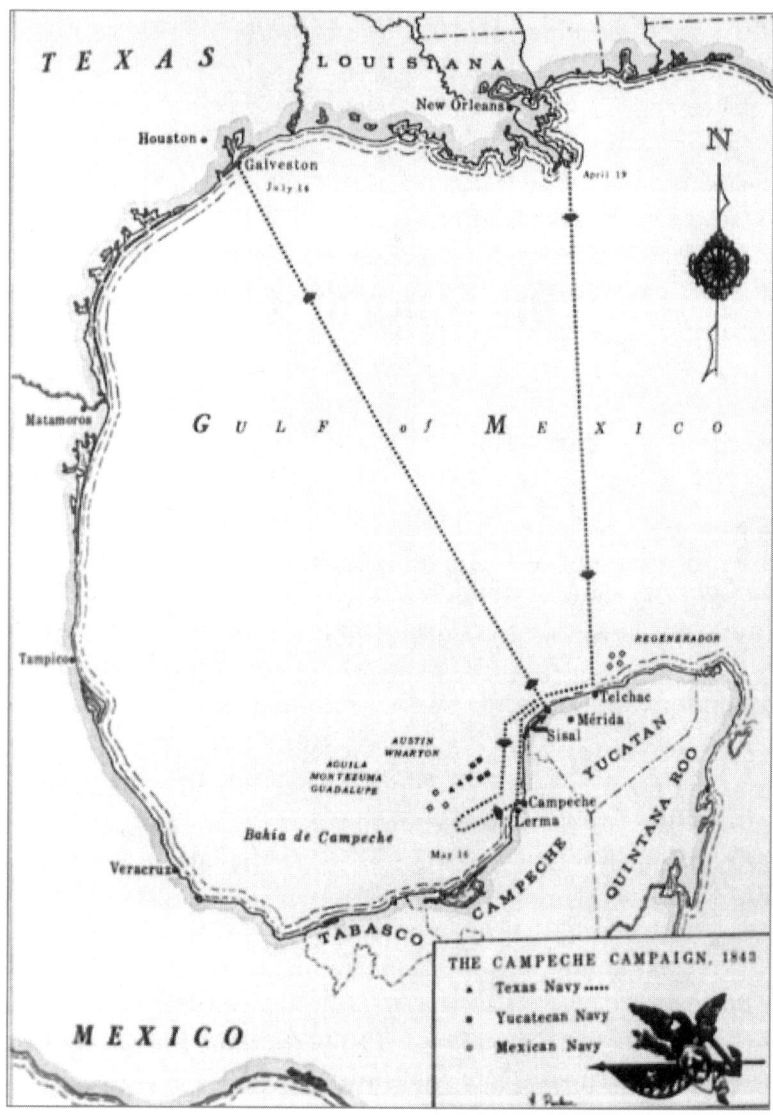

For a decade, 1832 to 1843, Texas fighting ships dominated the third coast of North America, the Gulf of Mexico, from New Orleans to the Yucatan. Their control of these waters was critical to the very existence of the struggling Texas Republic. (Texas State Historical Association, Austin)

virtually depopulated much of northern Mexico south of the Rio Grande.

Let the impulsive, well-armed gringos fight off those murderous hordes, they reasoned, and leave the provinces of Tamaulipas, Nuevo Leon, Coahuila, and Chihuahua in peace to grow and prosper.

In 1830, however, the Mexican government viewed with alarm the more than 30,000 *Americanos* who had settled from the Sabine River boundary with Louisiana, west to San Antonio, and along the Texas Gulf Coast. By the middle of that decade, American settlers outnumbered Mexican residents by ten to one.

There was a bright side, however; the Americans, called Texians, created thriving ports at Galveston, Brazoria, and Velasco where valuable cargoes of Texas beef, hides, corn, and cotton were shipped, mainly to New Orleans. In return they received manufactured goods from both the United States and Great Britain. Mexico City, which had only rarely extended any services to the colonists, now saw a rich source of revenue.

On April 6, 1830, they banned further immigration from the United States and sent tax collectors to Texas ports to levy duties on the rich export and import trade.

The Texians and the Tejanos, Mexicans living in Texas, were infuriated by the new controls. While the Texians muttered about taxation without representation, the Tejanos were equally livid. For the first time they had a market for their growing herds of longhorn cattle, and now a corrupt government was planning to steal a good portion of it. They complained that Mexico City had not only failed to protect them from Indian attacks, they even refused to send them priests so that their daughters could be legally married. Their government's response to the growing unrest of

Chapter 1

both groups was to send in soldiers to protect the tax collectors.

Further inflaming matters, Mexico City picked two autocratic, dishonest martinets to enforce the new tax laws. To administer the customhouse at Galveston they selected George Fisher, a Serb, who had fled to Italy after a failed revolt against the Turkish sultan. He became a mercenary soldier in Italy, wandering through the Danubian countries until, in 1815, he embarked for Philadelphia and later became an American citizen. Still suffering from wanderlust, he turned up in Mexico in 1821 to fight in one of the successful Mexican rebellions. As a reward for his services and because he spoke passable English, he was awarded the Galveston post.

At Anahuac, a small community at the far northeast end of Galveston Bay (an area now called Trinity Bay), he established a customhouse where he collected duties on all shipping passing through the bay area. Anahuac was located on a bank thirty feet above the waterline. From there one could view the bay more than twenty miles across, and on a clear day the brown smudge that was Galveston Island could be seen sixty miles to the southwest. Located near the mouth of the Trinity River, Anahuac was a community of several dozen log houses occupied by vigorous and ambitious merchants.

Autocratic, domineering, and arbitrary, Fisher's high-handed methods soon drove the Texians either to despair or to murderous frenzy. The water-borne commerce with which he was interfering was the economic life's blood of the Texas settlements and the sole source of income for the colonists.

Unlike most of the American western states, in the early days of Texas settlement, American immigrants did not enter the country by long journeys in covered wagons.

George Fisher, a Serb in Mexican service, established a custom post at Anahuac. Autocratic, domineering, and arbitrary, his high-handed methods drove the Texans to rebellion. (Texas State Library and Archives Commission)

Chapter 1

Trudging over the few rough trails that were subject to flooding and Indian attacks was slow, expensive, and dangerous. They came mostly by swift schooners, departing New Orleans and arriving at Galveston. After disembarking there, some transferred to smaller Gulf Coast packet boats for the more shallow passages past the barrier islands into Matagorda and Velasco.

Since the settlers considered the new taxes unfair, they were not shy about evading the law. Smuggling became a means of continuing the growing commerce, and soon schooner captains considered dodging the Mexican patrols a profitable form of sport.

They stopped smiling, however, when Fisher's *soldados* seized the Texian schooner *Canon* at the mouth of the Brazos River as it attempted to slip past the garrison at Velasco. Customs men boarded the ship and confiscated a contraband cargo of Texas-grown tobacco. It has almost become an axiom that revolutions often begin when middle-class merchants are hit in the pocketbook. So it was with Texas.

Other seizures followed. Forty pairs of men's shoes of American manufacture were seized on June 2, 1830, followed more ominously by the seizure of "eight sacks of ammunition" smuggled in from waters off Matagorda Island. As the confiscations increased, tempers rose to a boil.

On December 15, 1831, a Texian ship owner, Edwin Waller, ordered the skipper of his schooner *Sabine*, Captain Jeremiah Brown, to run past the Mexican customs port at Velasco. Ships like the *Sabine* were typical of the craft that plied the Texas coastal waters.

Similar Gulf Coast schooners usually had two masts and were fore-and-aft rigged, that is, the sails were secured to booms so that when sailing upwind they roughly paralleled the line between the bow and stern of the ship. This gave them the ability to sail close to the direction of the wind and maneuver quickly in shifting coastal winds. They were shallow draft, enabling them to sail in the shoal waters surrounding the Texas barrier islands and river inlets. Also, schooner-rigged ships, even with large sail areas, could be handled by a small crew.

Preparing to run past the fort, Captain Brown ordered the crew to pile bales of cotton along the taffrail, at the stern of the ship, to protect them from gunfire from the batteries adjacent to the customhouse.

Under a hail of gunfire, the *Sabine* sailed past the Velasco fort as bullets thudded harmlessly into the tight-packed cotton bales. On Waller's instructions, Captain Brown purchased two brass cannon in New Orleans and smuggled them back into the hands of the colonists on the return trip.

But if Fisher was bad, Colonel John Davis Bradburn, commanding the Mexican troops, was worse. A Kentuckian who also won acclaim serving in the revolutionary Mexican army, he had a shadowy and unsavory past. He fled from the United States after he and his brother were arrested and thrown into prison in Columbia, Tennessee, charged with stealing slaves. It was a charge that would reappear in later years and would dim his already shady reputation.

The Bradburn brothers planned to escape from jail after a confederate smuggled a file into their cell. On one moonless night the brothers sawed through their cell's bars and fled into the darkness. During a pursuit by Tennessee lawmen, his brother drowned, but Bradburn managed to wend his way to the Mississippi River and traveled downstream to New Orleans where he took a ship to Mexico.

There, he joined the Mexican army and fought with distinction against the Spaniards. His long service was

Chapter 1

rewarded with a colonel's rank and command of the soldiery in the Texas coastal areas.

Bradburn was an appropriate officer for the several hundred troops under his command. The Mexican law of September 29, 1826, provided for the enlistment of convicts as soldiers, and Bradburn's men were the sweepings of the scum of Mexican jails. There was a bad joke about a Mexican garrison commander who wrote to his headquarters, "I'm returning the shackles, please use them to send me more reinforcements."

In the fall of 1831, alarmed at the constant smuggling and not a few skirmishes between his garrisons and the Texians, Bradburn arbitrarily closed all Texas ports except Galveston. When the colonists protested, he declared martial law. According to the Texans, Bradburn was arbitrary, mean, a liar, and his pretentiousness made him the butt of ridicule. Even as mild-mannered a man as Texas empresario Stephen F. Austin said, "He was half crazy."

The order closing the ports was soon rescinded, but Bradburn's arbitrary methods of tax collecting were driving even heretofore honest Texas merchants into smuggling. Samuel Rhoads Fisher, who came to Texas in 1831 and organized a shipping business in the Matagorda Bay area, advised Stephen F. Austin of the threat to Texas commerce.

"Unless the laws are changed, it will be impossible for any vessel to carry on business in this area. Unless a change be made trade must be abandoned," he wrote. Already, he warned, Texas merchants were openly refusing to pay Bradburn's levies.

The ill will of the Texians turned into open rebellion over two incidents in May 1832. The first occurred when several of Bradburn's convict soldiers attacked and raped an American woman.

Opening Guns at Anahuac

As the drunken thugs grabbed the woman and started ripping off her clothes, she fought back, screaming loudly. A nearby American heard her cries but, afraid of the soldiers, refused to come to her aid. When the Texans learned of the attack, they first seized the cowardly American, stripped him naked, and soaked him in a bath of hot tar. Then they applied several coats of chicken feathers, forced him to straddle a fence rail, and rode him through the town, hooting and hollering. They called the ride "equestrian recreation for a scoundrel." Texans, then and now, have little patience with cowards.

Hearing the commotion, a Mexican lieutenant and four soldiers ran from their fort to quell the disturbance, but the infuriated Texans drove them off with a hail of rocks.

One of the leaders of the mob was a twenty-three-year-old firebrand of a lawyer named William Barret Travis, formerly of South Carolina, and later to achieve undying fame as the commander of the doomed Alamo. Flamboyant, wearing a broad-brimmed white planter's hat and flaming red pantaloons, he soon became a leader among the Texans who were dubbed "The War Party."

When Bradburn refused to punish the soldiers, Travis took part in organizing a militia company, which he maintained was formed to protect the settlers from Indian attacks. Bradburn, no fool, realized the company was designed to smash him and his garrison.

But venality overcame caution, and the colonel triggered a situation that led to what one colonist claimed was the first action of the Texas navy.

The issue involved slavery, a problem that would haunt Texas for three decades. The Mexican government forbade slavery in its provinces, but because the Mexican economy was dependent on debt peonage, an equally degrading

Chapter 1

system, they turned a blind eye when emigrating Americans brought their slaves into Texas.

Bradburn was in the habit of compelling colonists' slaves to construct public works without compensation to the owners. He also told some runaway slaves working on the waterfront that if they asked for protection under the laws of Mexico, he would set them free. Three runaways took him up on his boast, but instead of freeing them, the colonel put the men to work on personal projects, refusing to return them to their owner.

Lawyer Travis, representing the owner, exchanged heated words with the slippery colonel, and Bradburn later claimed that Travis threatened his life. He was probably correct. The following day, while Travis and Pat Jack, a fellow lawyer who was active in the militia, were working in their office, a squad of Mexican soldiers with fixed bayonets flung open their door and placed them under arrest. The two lawyers were hauled to the jail at Anahuac and tossed into a cell.

The jail, situated near the mouth of the Trinity River about a mile and a half from the village, was a half-finished building constructed of local bricks. The two incarcerated Southern gentlemen, fed on a diet of stale bread and boiled beans, were forced to complete the construction of their prison. Under close guard they were put to work tramping clay and molding bricks, which were fired in a nearby kiln.

Considerably muddied, the two brick makers sent out their laundry by way of a friend's slave. The suspicious Bradburn, rummaging through their dirty shirts, found a note stating, "Have a horse in readiness Thursday night." Alarmed, Bradburn doubled the guard and primed two iron 6-pounder cannon in front of the jail doorway.

Meanwhile, Pat Jack's brother William, infuriated by the jailing and determined to free the two Texans, called out the militia. When 150 armed settlers appeared before the jail and offered to exchange fifteen of Bradburn's cavalrymen they had captured in exchange for Travis and Jack, the colonel, cursing the men, refused.

His soldiers dragged the two Anglos from their cell and shackled them to the floor of the jail. Bradburn shouted, "If you fire upon us, I will kill them." Travis, unafraid, hollered back, "Shoot, my friends. I would rather die a thousand deaths than permit this oppressor to remain unpunished."

The Texans took him at his word and opened up a deadly hail of rifle fire against the jail. Bradburn abruptly changed his mind and agreed to a swap as Texan bullets began pock marking the jail wall, smashing windows, and riddling the door. The gullible militiamen ceased firing, turned over their prisoners, and waited for the release of Travis and Jack. Instead, the colonel slammed the jail door and opened fire on the Texans. He soon learned, however, that his treachery was a mistake.

Within minutes, horsemen galloped throughout the Texian settlements shouting, "To arms! To arms! Take your rifle and ride to Anahuac. Free our men from the claws of rascally and convict soldiers who guard the jail at Anahuac."

Hundreds of settlers downed their ploughs, picked up their squirrel rifles or shotguns, and rode or hiked along dusty trails to the port town. Within forty-eight hours more than 300 armed men arrived and besieged Bradburn's garrison. After a brisk exchange of gunfire killed five soldiers and one colonist, the Texan leaders sent a messenger to Brazoria urging the settlers there to bring three brass cannon in their possession to Anahuac. The cannon, they believed, would provide enough firepower to blast down the jail's brick walls.

Chapter 1

From the upper reaches of the Brazos River north of Brazoria, a shallow-draft schooner named the *Brazoria* was sailed down to the town dock, and the cannon were loaded aboard. When the Mexican commander of the fort at Velasco refused to let the schooner pass under their guns into the Gulf of Mexico, the Texans mounted their brass cannon into firing position on the schooner's deck. They piled cotton bales around the bulwarks and boarded forty picked men armed with deadly, long-range Kentucky rifles.

Sailing downstream, the heavily loaded schooner soon ran aground on a Brazos River mud bank. Cursing, the men piled out into the thigh-deep water and unloaded the guns. Straining mightily, they rocked the boat and heaved on a stout anchor line until they hauled the *Brazoria* into deeper water. Then they reloaded the guns and rode the river current down to the Mexican fort at Velasco.

At midnight, June 26, 1832, under full sail and with weapons primed, they slipped up near the fort while another group of Texans approached from landward. After the land-based Texans opened fire, the *Brazoria* dropped anchor 150 yards off the fort and began a cannonade.

The fort was a formidable structure. It consisted of a wall constructed of sharpened, upright logs that formed a circular redoubt. More logs and heaped sand piled up against the wall reinforced the palisade against rifle and cannon fire. At the center of the fort was a high log bastion upon which a 9-pounder swivel gun was mounted. A smaller swivel gun was mounted on the parapet of the wall near the front gate. The weakness in the design was that the Mexican artillerymen were left unprotected from the fire of the Kentucky rifles in the hands of the Texas marksmen.

During the hot, steamy night, the *Brazoria*'s gun crews rammed powder charges, then rifle balls, scrap iron, and even rocks down the cannon's mouths and blasted away.

The Texans' most formidable adversaries that night were the swarms of huge, bloodthirsty, Gulf Coast mosquitoes launching their own attack against the bared skin of the gunners.

The fighting continued until 2 o'clock in the morning when a squall roared in from the Gulf. The heavy rains soaked the flintlocks and percussion caps of the rifles and muskets on both sides, and the land campaign fizzled out in the dampness.

The cannon of the fort and the schooner were unaffected by the rain, and their firing continued until dawn. But while the Mexican gunners failed to hit the anchored schooner, the *Brazoria*'s few large cannon balls and hails of smaller shot smashed up the fort's thin palisade of vertical logs.

Shortly before dawn the *Brazoria*'s moorings gave way either from the effects of the rainstorm or Mexican shot. With an outgoing tide the ship drifted toward the fort, running aground about 100 yards from the stockade.

When the rain stopped, with the morning light the lethal Texas riflemen on both land and water began to pick off Mexican soldiers with devastating accuracy. The men on the *Brazoria*, protected by the cotton bales and braced against them for steady shooting, created particular havoc among the Mexican cannoneers attempting to fire the swivel gun.

As their comrades were shot down, other Mexican soldiers bravely leaped to service the guns until they in turn were hit by the fire of the deadly Texas riflemen.

Soon a white flag fluttering from a thin sapling waved over the battered walls. The inside of the fort resembled a charnel house with bleeding and dying men either praying to the Virgin, crying for their mothers, or cursing the damned Texians. The garrison of 150 suffered thirty-five

Chapter 1

dead and fifteen wounded. The Texans had seven killed and twenty-seven wounded among those who attacked from the land. None of the schooner's crew was injured. The Mexican garrison was allowed to march out with the honors of war although they were ordered to leave their cannon and swivel gun behind.

It was a lame march, more of a stagger, as the shocked troops, carrying their wounded on makeshift and blood-soaked litters, wended their way to the causeway and boarded a Mexican ship to take them away from the accursed land of Texas.

As the *Brazoria* was preparing to set sail for Anahuac, the Texans received word that Bradburn had surrendered and their guns were not needed.

While the fight at Velasco was reaching its climax, Robert M. Williamson, a friend of Travis who was also a lawyer and militia officer, led another group of armed Texans against the fortified Anahuac jail. Known throughout the Anglo settlements as "Three-Legged Willie," he was a handsome young man and a dynamic lawyer who had suffered a childhood illness that left him with a crippled right leg. The leg had stiffened and bent back at a ninety-degree angle from the knee. Williamson had a peg leg attached to the knee joint, and with his good leg and a cane he could stump around a courtroom with amazing agility. The bent leg, stockinged and shoed, however, proved somewhat disconcerting to some courtroom visitors.

Three-Legged Willie, Travis, and Pat Jack were a fun-loving, party-giving, and hard-drinking trio. While Travis and Jack danced wild fandangos with both the señoritas and Anglo lasses of the settlements, Willie provided the music, strumming his banjo and singing love songs in both Spanish and English.

Opening Guns at Anahuac

Robert M. "Three-Legged Willie" Williamson, nicknamed for his artificial leg, did not allow his handicap to stifle his championship of the Texas cause. (Texas State Library and Archives

Chapter 1

Willie's men combined forces with other Texans under the command of Colonel F.W. Johnson. During a council of war the men realized that they must command the waters of Galveston Bay if they were to lay a successful siege to the Anahuac jail. To that end they engaged three small shallow draft schooners, the *Stephen F. Austin*, *Water Witch*, and *Red River*.

Fitting them out with provisions, guns, and ammunition, they began a blockade of Galveston Bay, both to prevent the prisoners from being spirited away and to stop provisions and reinforcements from reaching Bradburn. It was Texas's first flotilla.

The *Stephen F. Austin* and the *Red River* were five-tonners, each carrying a crew of five. One man sailed while the others served the swivel guns or small cannon mounted on the boats. The *Water Witch* was a half-ton lighter and carried four men armed with rifles.

As they patrolled the murky waters, they put sharp-eyed lookouts in their bows to spot the semi-submerged logs and trees being washed down from the Trinity River, which in turn emptied into the bay near Anahuac. There were other hazards, for the dark-colored shallow waters concealed mud flats that could strand even a flat-bottomed schooner. There were also treacherous oyster reefs whose sharp-edged shells could grind out the bottom of a wooden boat.

Cruising by the mostly uninhabited shores and on the unspoiled waters that summer presented to the Texas sailors the glorious sight of thousands of gaily plumaged birds flying and fishing over the sun-sparkled waters. Spoonbills, blue and white herons, egrets, snipe, sandpipers, loons, gulls, terns, and the comically ungainly pelicans dived and swooped. On the lower bay a trio of playful dolphins was likely to dive under one side of the boat and come up grinning on the other. But it was not all fun and games.

Captain David L. Kokernot, skipper of the *Red River*, learned about the Texas coast the hard way. Born in Holland in 1805, he settled in New Orleans where he became a federal revenue officer. While chasing smugglers in 1831, his ship was wrecked off the Texas coast during a storm. He managed to make it to shore, hiked to Anahuac, and so liked the area that after he reached New Orleans he moved his family to that struggling small port. There, he captained coastal schooners in the New Orleans trade.

He later wrote, "We had a perfect blockade, so that no one could carry provisions to the enemy and we had no little sport running near enough to the fort to provoke the fire of the enemy's guns. "Fortunately," he said, "They couldn't hit us."

He recounted, "We captured three boats as prizes, loaded with provisions such as butter, eggs, chickens, beef and pork, besides all sorts of dainties and you may be sure we lived high on those provisions."

Throughout June the small flotilla continued to cruise up and down Galveston Bay and the mouth of the Trinity River. The *Stephen F. Austin* captured a prize carrying beef and cornmeal for the fort at Double Bayou. Near Cedar Point the *Water Witch* overtook and seized two Mexican schooners loaded with food for the garrison.

To many Mexican officers, however, the siege of Anahuac was a mere sideshow to a revolution that suddenly swept over Mexico. During 1832 General Antonio Lopez de Santa Anna launched a revolt against the government in Mexico City, which he claimed had destroyed the democratic constitution of 1824.

With Mexico wracked with rebellion, Mexican Colonel José de Las Piedras, sent to reinforce Bradburn, feared a general uprising among the Texans. To ease tensions he met with a delegation of American colonists at the small settlement of Liberty. There he agreed to free Travis and Jack, restore personal properties seized by Bradburn, and relieve the obnoxious colonel from his command.

On July 2 Travis and Jack were freed and greeted as heroes by an exuberant crowd of Texans. That same night, under cover of darkness, Bradburn saddled a horse, slipped out of Anahuac, and rode furiously until he reached the safety of the Louisiana border. His escape frustrated the Texans, many of whom devoutly wished to hang him from the highest tree in Anahuac.

Captain Kokernot sailed the *Red River* down to Galveston where his armed crew captured the customhouse and all its impounded goods without losing a man. Proudly he announced, "We were the first Texas Navy."

Colonel Piedras, sensing the hostility of the Texans, evacuated Mexican garrisons at Nacogdoches and the upper Brazos. With the surrender of the garrisons at Velasco, Anahuac, and Galveston, there were no longer any Mexican soldiers on Texian territory.

On the larger scene, Santa Anna's revolutionary movement succeeded and he seized the reins of government in Mexico City. In an act of inspired chutzpah, Three-Legged Willie informed the new government that the affairs at Anahuac were not a revolt against Mexican sovereignty. The Texans, he said, were showing support for General Santa Anna and the liberal, democratic constitution of 1824. It is doubtful if anyone in Mexico City was fooled.

CHAPTER 2

Clashes at Sea

A quiet interlude reigned along the Texas Gulf Coast as commerce increased between Texas and American ports. In October 1832 the Texans held a convention that approved resolutions petitioning Mexico for both statehood and abolition of all tariffs.

The tariff resolution was somewhat pro forma because all customs officers were driven out during the previous disturbances, and the Texans enjoyed a laissez-faire commerce that would have gladdened the heart of Adam Smith. From 1832 until 1835 there were neither Mexican troops nor Mexican authority north of the Rio Grande. Unfortunately, the good times, when Texas and American ships sailed past deserted customs stations and abandoned forts, were not to last.

Santa Anna, feeling secure in Mexico City, began flexing his muscles and tightening his grip on all of Mexico. During this time, in the spring of 1833, mild-mannered Stephen F. Austin journeyed to Mexico City to present the request for Texas statehood. The petition was not only rejected but

Chapter 2

Austin was arrested and thrown in prison on suspicion of fomenting rebellion.

Stephen F. Austin was a loyal citizen of Mexico until Santa Anna threw him in prison and seized dictatorial powers. Disillusioned, Austin joined forces with the Texas "War Party." (Texas State Library and Archives Commission)

Santa Anna jailed the wrong man; he should have arrested William Barret Travis.

In May 1834 Santa Anna shook off all pretense of liberalism and democracy and announced his *Plan de Cuernavaca*, which centralized power into his egocentric hands. Early in 1835 he sent a strong garrison of soldiers to San Antonio. Worse, from the merchants' point of view, he re-established customhouses at Anahuac, Brazoria, and Galveston. He also constructed a prison at each location.

Adding insult to injury, he ordered the schooner-of-war *Moctezuma* to patrol the Texas coast and seize traders who evaded customs duties. Since this included almost all the ships entering or leaving Texas ports, merchants and ship owners were aghast that their right to smuggle was being abridged.

The Gulf Coast calm was quickly shattered when a Texas smuggler captain found a Mexican customs official traveling as a passenger on his ship. He confronted the man at gunpoint, forced him over the side, and marooned him on one of the barrier islands. After living a Robinson Crusoe existence for days, the man was finally rescued by a fishing boat. It was not an incident that aided in relieving the growing tension between Texas settlers and Mexican bureaucrats.

On land the rambunctious Texans refused to sell the Mexican garrisons meat, bread, or vegetables. One night after the garrison commander at Anahuac assembled a huge pile of cut lumber to rebuild the old fort there, a bold Texan slipped past the sentry and set the lumber ablaze.

When the Mexican customs collector at Anahuac threw an unruly Texan into jail, the ever-inflammatory William Barret Travis, then residing at nearby Harrisburg, decided on strong action. Commanding a force of fifty militiamen, he ordered a 6-pounder cannon to be mounted on truck

Chapter 2

wheels that were normally used for hauling logs to a sawmill. The men pulled the cannon to the waterfront and hoisted it aboard the schooner *Ohio*, which immediately set sail for Anahuac. Upon arrival, the militia attacked and captured the fort, released the prisoner, and forced the abandonment of the post.

The tempo of events quickened along the coast in June when the *Moctezuma* seized the Texan-owned coaster *Martha* as it was skimming along the barrier islands with a cargo of smuggled goods. After a shot across her bow caused *Martha* to turn into the wind and haul down her sails, Mexican seamen boarded the vessel. They imprisoned her crew in a hold and sailed *Martha* into the port of Matamoros at the mouth of the Rio Grande. Upon docking there, they ensconced the Texas crew in the local jail.

At this time the United States revenue ship *Ingham* was anchored off the port with the crew ashore, filling its casks with fresh water.

The *Ingham* was one of a series of revenue ships built in 1830 for the high speed needed to run down smugglers and pirates. A topsail schooner, she displaced 112 tons.

Her mainmast and foremast supported three square-cut sails suspended from wooden yards set horizontally across the mast. These sails gave the ship drive when the wind was blowing from astern or on the quarter.

There were three or more long triangular jib sails set forward of the mast and stretched to the bowsprit, a long wooden spar extending from the bow. These sails enabled the ship to sail close to the wind and maneuver quickly, an important capability in tricky coastal waters.

The mizzenmast, shorter and set behind the main mast, was gaff rigged. The gaff sail was rectangular and was hoisted by an attached spar called a gaff. It was attached at the bottom to a wooden boom controlled by several lines (ropes to the layman). Set at a right angle to its mast, the sail could be shifted from side to side to aid in maneuverability. When pulled in close it helped the ship sail close to the wind. When the wind was behind or on the quarter, it could be let out, giving a large driving force to the ship.

The *Ingham*'s rig was a popular rig for ships expected to sail close inshore as well as on the open sea. Seventy-three feet long, she had a shallow draft of ten feet. She was manned by a crew of twenty-four and carried four 9-pounder guns mounted fore or aft or between the masts. The guns were often placed on circular mounts that gave them a wide arc of fire.

The *Ingham*'s captain, a belligerent old sea dog named Ezekiel Jones, was always spoiling for a fight with smugglers, slavers, privateers, pirates, or anyone foolish enough to engage him. He was one of those old-time skippers whose tactics were, "Give 'em two broadsides and board 'em in the smoke."

Knowing his temperament, Texas merchants, with Machiavellian guile, approached Jones while he was ashore and convinced him that although the *Martha* was Texan owned, she was registered in the United States. As such, they said, she was an American ship.

"The flag of the United States has been insulted and an American ship has been illegally seized and an American crew has been falsely imprisoned," they complained. "What are you going to do to resolve this injustice?" they asked.

Jones would do plenty, he promised. He summoned his master-of-arms and ordered him to round up his crew, still on shore leave. The master-of-arms and a boatswain scoured the grog shops and whorehouses of Matamoros, rounded up the crew, and brought them forthwith to the American ship.

Chapter 2

As the fuzzy-brained seamen reached the ship and busied themselves hauling up the anchor and raising sail, Captain Jones spotted the *Moctezuma* sailing out of the port into the open sea. With thunderous curses from the captain and the application of the mate's knotted line to the rear ends of the still groggy crew, the *Ingham* was soon underway and in hot pursuit of the Mexican man-o-war.

At dawn on June 14, 1835, a lookout in the crow's nest spotted the sail tops of the Mexican ship, and Jones piled on every sail on the ship. He didn't have to hurry, for at the same moment the *Moctezuma* spotted the *Ingham*. Believing she was another Texas smuggler, the Mexican ship turned downwind and bore down upon the American with her guns run out and ready to fire.

When both ships were within several hundred yards of each other, the *Moctezuma* opened fire with her bow chaser cannon, but missed. The *Ingham*, beating against the wind, then performed the classic naval maneuver called "crossing the T" as Captain Jones shouted, "Hoist the ensign. Run out the guns." Then he gave the command, "Prepare to go about" and "helm's alee" and with a rush of sails the ship executed a 90-degree turn.

With the Stars and Stripes streaming in the breeze, the four 6-pounder guns loaded with solid shot, and a captain almost salivating with delight, the *Ingham* crossed the bow of the Mexican ship. Jones yelled "Fire" and all four guns blasted the *Moctezuma*'s foredeck, holing sails, smashing spars, and bloodying the crew.

Suddenly realizing he was up against an armed American warship, the Mexican skipper, deciding discretion was the better part of valor, made a run back to Matamoros. For six and a half hours the *Ingham* kept up a hot pursuit.

As the Mexican ship closed the harbor, its captain realized the *Ingham* was overtaking them and was about to come within gun range. Throwing caution, literally, to the winds, he raced into the harbor and, trying to cross the bar, ran hard aground.

When the American cutter fired its forward gun and its plummeting shot sent a geyser spraying the stern of the stranded ship, the captain screamed, "Throw everything overboard."

The frantic crew dumped guns, cannonballs, anchors, water casks, buckets of nails, kegs of gunpowder, and anything not nailed down, over the side. Thus lightened, the *Moctezuma* rose with a few feet of water under her keel, slipped over the bar, and found refuge in the port.

Captain Jones sailed his ship over the bar, dropped anchor, and trained his guns on the harbormaster's office. Ever bellicose, he was rowed ashore and demanded the release of the "American sailors and the American ship." Observing the *Ingham*'s gun crews standing by their weapons with smoldering matches and eager looks, the harbormaster readily agreed. He not only released the prisoners, surrendered the *Martha*, and made profuse apologies but also gave the cowed *Moctezuma* captain a profane chewing out. Within a short time the *Ingham* and the *Martha*, with all pennants flying, sailed triumphantly out of Matamoros harbor.

The spectacle of the Texans laughing at the discomfit of the Mexican navy only widened the ever-growing breach between the Anglo settlers and the government in Mexico City.

After the humiliation of the *Moctezuma*, an infuriated Santa Anna sent three warships, the *Josefa, Ana Maria,* and the *Correo de Mexico*, to the Texas Gulf Coast. Lacking experienced seamen, Santa Anna began a policy of hiring British naval officers who had either left the service or who were on half-pay, extended leave status.

Chapter 2

One such officer was Thomas M. Thompson. An example of waterfront flotsam, he served in his Britannic Majesty's navy, drifted into New Orleans, operated a seamy grog house, and later wandered into Mexico. There, his expertise gained him a commission as a *Teniente Segundo de Marina* in the navy of the Republic of Mexico and the command of the *Correo de Mexico*.

A slightly built, mild-looking man, Thompson made up for his mediocre appearance by always bellowing commands in broken Spanish and exercising a nasty temper on all occasions. He was a man with a passionate desire to enrich himself at the expense of the Texans.

Given command of the *Correo de Mexico* and ordered to destroy the smugglers and revolting mobs in the Galveston area, he sailed into the bay during the summer of 1835. Finding the Mexican customhouse abandoned after Travis's attack, Thompson issued a draconian proclamation on July 26. "The militia of Anahuac is to be disbanded or I will burn down the town," he ordered. Then he arbitrarily seized a Texas sloop and other property as he patrolled the Texas coast like a hungry vulture.

It was a long and hard coast to patrol. The 370 miles of Texas coastline are laced with sand spits, oyster reefs, estuaries, lagoons, and narrow, shallow inlets. A series of sandy barrier islands stretch from the Sabine River border with Louisiana to the mouth of the Rio Grande River and the state of Tamaulipas. Padre Island, the southernmost island stretches for 113 miles, making it the longest barrier island on earth.

The coastal waters, fed by Texas rivers, are mud brown, sluggish, and murky for miles offshore. Treacherous sandbars, lurking only eight to twelve feet below the surface, hampered the passage of heavily laden ships attempting to enter Texas harbors. Running aground while trying to cross the bar was an ever-present hazard.

The barrier islands provided some protection from Gulf Coast storms for the small ports of Velasco and Brazosport and enabled landings at the many sheltered shallow water lagoons. Entries through breaks in the barrier island chain were treacherous as their channels often silted up or shifted following a storm.

Even a shallow draft ship, before entering, had to send out a small boat. The boatmen, using long poles or a weighted line, would search for the channel by probing the water depth. When they located a channel deeper than their ship's draft they marked it using a system of floating corks or wooden buoys. The channel markers were held in place by a line with an attached weight that would anchor it to the bottom.

Theoretically, the ship could follow the markers to a safe anchorage in the lagoon or improvised port jetty. It was a slow, tedious procedure, and it had to be repeated at each entry as tides, currents, or bad weather would cause the markers to break loose or shift their position.

Galveston was the only reliable deep-water port for large seagoing ships on the Texas coast. British traveler William Bollaert described the city, a former lair for the notorious pirate Jean Lafitte, as containing "a motley mixture of freebooters and smugglers, under the Mexican flag."

The island is a flat sandy beach nearly thirty miles long and from one to two miles in breadth. While it is denuded of trees and all but a few shrubs, Bollaert wrote, "The bayous and ponds are full of alligators and snakes. Mosquitoes in myriads."

For all that, Galveston began to boom when Austin's colonists started to arrive in large numbers and commerce in cattle and cotton began to increase. Bollaert wrote that by

Chapter 2

May 1839, "There were 30 sailings in the harbor...three steamers were plying regularly between it and New Orleans and the same numbers between it and Houston."

From the beginnings of the thirst for Texas independence, Galveston was the key to the survival of a free republic. But there was always danger.

Texas port cities are only fifteen to twenty feet above sea level and from July through October are at risk from being destroyed by the hurricanes that periodically ravage the coast. And any ship caught in hurricane winds and waves is likely to make a rapid trip to Davy Jones' Gulf Coast locker.

In 1839 Galveston was the leading port in Texas and became the home base of the republic's navy. Holding Galveston and securing the safety of

Clashes at Sea

The sudden, squally summer storms with heavy southerly winds could drive the most weatherly vessel inshore to be battered into debris by the relentless waves pounding it into the sandy beaches or grinding it into lurking oyster reefs.

The winter months offered no surcease from danger as the dreaded "northers" swept down from the mainland, bringing whipping winds, freezing temperatures, sleet, and sometimes hailstones as big as eggs. The driving winds of those storms could break anchor lines and propel a ship out to sea to vanish in a shroud of darkened clouds and hammering rain.

the seaborne trade through New Orleans was essential to the survival of the young republic. (Texas State Library and Archives Commission)

Chapter 2

Testimony to the caprice of Texas weather are the bleached timbers, looking like so many nautical skeletons, that are seen littering the sun-blasted sandy isles.

Roaming the beach areas were myriads of wildlife, hundreds of species of birds, rabbits, deer, turkeys, and seemingly armies of defiant rattlesnakes.

Sailors shipwrecked on the islands could dine comfortably, cooking oysters, shrimp, and assorted fish and game over driftwood fires. On these delicacies they could survive, providing, of course, a hurricane didn't drown them, a rattlesnake didn't poison them, or one of the few surviving Karankawa Indians didn't eat them.

Defying these dangers, on the morning outgoing tide of October 1, 1835, the merchant brig *Tremont* departed the port of Velasco loaded with a cargo of pine and cedar lumber. The merchantman passed over the bar at the mouth of the Brazos River and sailed close-hauled on a course for Pensacola.

With little wind in a mild seaway, she wallowed toward the southeast. She was easy pickings for "Mexico" Thompson and the *Correo de Mexico*. The Britisher overtook her, fired a shot across her bow, and when the *Tremont* went dead in the water, he led a boarding party aboard her.

Not satisfied with the *Tremont*'s manifests, Thompson declared the cargo contraband, seized the ship, and imprisoned the crew below deck. He put an eight-man prize crew aboard with orders to sail the ship to Veracruz. Back aboard the *Correo*, Thompson spread all his canvas and attempted to beat further out to sea, but the wind died and both ships slopped about in the quiet waters of a dead calm.

In the meantime, a large group of Texans on the Velasco wharfs witnessed the *Tremont*'s capture. Swearing they would recover the ship, they grabbed their ever-present rifles and heavy-bladed butcher knives and piled into the

Laura, a small steam-driven coaster. With much clanking, banging, and whistling, the *Laura* got up steam and, with her decks laced with angry Texas riflemen, paddled out past the bar and into the Gulf waters.

Seeing the *Laura* chugging his way, the frustrated Thompson, still becalmed and drifting toward land, swept the horizon with his telescope and spotted a group of Texans wheeling up a brass cannon along the shoreline.

Within minutes Texas rifle balls from the *Laura* began to hole his sails and sent splinters flying from his bulwarks. Then with a loud boom the on-shore cannon sent an iron ball ripping through his canvas. Cursing, he signaled the prize crew aboard the *Tremont* to abandon the ship and row like hell back to the becalmed *Correo*.

As an incoming tide pushed the *Tremont* toward shore, the *Laura* chugged up, tossed a line to the now freed crew, and taking her in tow, headed back toward Velasco. Furious, Thompson ordered his gunners to open fire with the *Correo*'s swivel gun, but the two Texas ships were soon out of range.

At that moment, a new actor was about to enter the drama. Back in July when Thompson was threatening the settlers at Anahuac with arson, Stephen F. Austin was going aboard ship in Veracruz. Freed from imprisonment after two miserable years, he was en route to New Orleans and he was a changed man.

Before Santa Anna tossed him into jail, Austin had always been a loyal Mexican citizen, often cooling the tempers of the tempestuous Texans. His sole political ambition was to make Texas a state in the Mexican federation.

But during his imprisonment he watched the gaudy Santa Anna turn from a professed liberal to a wildly ambitious dictator and autocrat who crushed opposition with treachery and violence. Now, he believed, Texas had no

Chapter 2

choice; he would bow to the aims of Travis and his hot-headed friends. "Texas," he wrote, "must and ought to be a part of the United States of America."

Arriving in New Orleans in August, he purchased gunpowder and cannonballs and had them loaded onto the Texas-owned ship *San Felipe*. Then he ordered the ship to set sail for Brazoria. The *San Felipe* was under the command of hard-charging Captain W.A. Hurd, who was spoiling for a chance to fight a Mexican man-o-war.

Hurd was expecting trouble. He had mounted two 6-pounder cannon on his deck and surrounded them with thick cotton bales. Then he issued rifles and ammunition to his crew of Texans.

Just before they left port, a mysterious, cloaked passenger slipped aboard the vessel. He was later identified as the disenchanted former private secretary of Santa Anna, Don Lorenzo de Zavala. Within weeks Zavala would sign the Texas Declaration of Independence, and later he would be elected vice president of the independent Republic of Texas.

As fate would have it, the *San Felipe*, catching a fresh sea breeze, sailed into the Brazos waters in the middle of the gun battle between the Texans and the *Correo*. The captain of the *Laura*, meanwhile, after depositing the *Tremont* at the docks, spotted the *San Felipe*. The little steamer charged out to the Gulf and took *San Felipe* under tow. After being tugged across the bar, Austin, de Zavala, and other passengers were transferred to the steamer. In exchange, the armed volunteers aboard the *Laura* soon lined the decks of the *San Felipe* and began priming their rifles.

As the *Laura* chugged back to port, the *San Felipe* turned toward her foe. As the Texan ship hove into view, "Mexico" Thompson turned his attention to the new arrival. He slowly wore ship and in sluggish winds, sailed toward her with cannon primed.

It is possible that Thompson was alerted that the *San Felipe* was loaded with "hollowware," a euphemism for cannon, and other munitions, and he saw another opportunity for loot.

At eight o'clock in the fading twilight, the *Correo* came within range and without warning opened fire on the *San Felipe*. Unknowingly he had sailed into a hornet's nest of gunfire as the Texas ship carrying superior firepower hit back hard. Two 6-pounders in the waist along with a fusillade of rifle fire crashed into the Mexican ship. In the first salvo the *Correo*'s two cannon were dismounted, most of the crew wounded, and Thompson was struck in both legs by Texas rifle balls.

Realizing he had again overmatched himself, with holed sails and bleeding crew, Thompson slowly turned seaward in an effort to escape as the *San Felipe*'s gunfire continued to rake his ship.

In light winds, the two ships engaged in a slow-motion ballet as both vessels, flying everything but their captain's bedspreads, attempted to gain speed in the fading breeze.

For two hours at long range they cannonaded each other, doing little damage as they drifted apart. When night fell the firing stopped, and the two warring ships floated silently on the dark waters.

When dawn finally broke, both ships were still drifting aimlessly in the turgid sea, well out of gunshot range. Soon, however, Captain Hurd gave a loud hurrah when he spied the little steamer *Laura* chugging his way.

As *Laura* came alongside, laughing sailors tossed heavy lines to the Texas steamer. Then, paddlewheels churning, the *Laura* towed *San Felipe* toward the becalmed *Correo*. When they got within gun range, Captain Hurd gave the order to open fire. After their first volley raked the *Correo*

Chapter 2

killing a mate, "Mexico" Thompson raised a white flag to the masthead.

Captain Hurd and a boarding party climbed aboard the battered ship where they found the bodies of five sailors, killed in the battle, strewn on the deck. They promptly put Thompson and his surviving crew of two officers and fourteen seamen in chains. Hurd, in a bellowing voice, announced to the cowed men, "You are damned pirates and I'm taking you to New Orleans where you will be tried and hung."

After putting a prize crew aboard the *Correo*, the *San Felipe* unloaded passengers and cargo in Velasco and then both ships set a course for New Orleans.

In January 1836 "Mexico" Thompson and his first lieutenant, Carlos Ocampo, were tried on a charge of piracy in the Federal District Court of New Orleans. The high point in the trial occurred when Thompson's attorney, the Honorable P. Soule, and Federal District Attorney H. Carleton carried their legal arguments into the realm of personal abuse.

It is not recorded which attorney first threw the inkwell that splattered the fine clothes of his opponent. The other attorney obliged in kind, and soon husky bailiffs were obliged to pull apart the screaming, ink-splattered lawyers. When things calmed down the judge, who was not amused, ordered both men to spend six hours cooling off in a jail cell. After that interlude, the lawyers, with presumably clean shirts, continued the case.

When a representative of the Mexican government testified that Thompson and Ocampo were bona fide officers in the Mexican navy, the piracy charge was dropped and both men were set free. The *New Orleans Courier* newspaper commented on January 16, 1836, "It was a remarkable trial

...it never happened before...the pirates were set at liberty and the attorneys committed to jail."

The trial was also anti-climatic because, by early October of the previous year, total war had broken out between Texas and Santa Anna's Mexico.

Chapter 3

Of Privateers and Pirates

After landing at Brazoria, Stephen F. Austin rode to San Felipe where, in September 1835, he was elected chairman of a Committee of Safety. As the members were discussing Santa Anna's oppressive dictatorship, an exhausted rider dismounted from a sweat-lathered horse and dashed into the meeting. He brought the fateful news that General Martín Perfecto Cos had crossed the Rio Grande with a large force of soldiers and was advancing toward San Antonio. At the same time another message from Texan spies reported a battalion of the Mexican army had departed the port of Matamoros. They were reported to be sailing for the small port of Copano on the south Texas coast, which was reached by a narrow passage through Aransas Pass.

At the news, the formerly pacifistic Austin in an impassioned speech to cheering Texans declared, "War is our only resource. There is no other remedy. We must defend our rights, ourselves, and our country by force of arms."

Another more sobering report stated Cos was carrying 800 sets of manacles to be used in dragging Texas rebels across the desert to Mexico City where they would be executed.

On October 2 fighting broke out between Texas militiamen and the Mexican army at the little town of Gonzales, and the war was on. Desperate for arms, Texas patriots rejoiced when on October 26 the privateer *San Felipe*, which had loaded a cargo of rifles, ammunition, and cannon in New Orleans, arrived in Galveston. On November 3 a Texas provisional government was formed, and one of the first items on the agenda was how to protect their lifeblood of commerce along the Gulf Coast.

These farsighted Texans understood the vital necessity for sea power. More than half a century later their earlier vision was justified when the great American naval strategist Admiral Alfred T. Mahan declared that the surest deterrent to invasion from the Gulf of Mexico was "a fleet of swift cruisers to prey on the enemy's commerce."

The men of the new government realized that if Texas warships could prevent the reinforcement of the Mexican armies by sea, they could strangle Santa Anna's invasion force. If the sea route was closed, the Mexicans would have to trudge more than 200 miles from their nearest land base at Monclova to San Antonio. It would be a least a twelve-day march across arid land, with sparse forage. What passed for roads were mere trails, usually choked with dust except during the rare rains when they became muddy quagmires. Exhausted Mexicans later named their overland route of advance the "Desert of Dead Horses."

Mexican transport consisted of either *carretas*, wagons with two huge wooden wheels usually pulled by oxen or mules, or pack trains of small, heavily loaded burros. Through sparsely settled South Texas it was not possible for an army to live off the land.

Chapter 3

The lack of forage and water for the animals was bad enough, but the tortoise-like speed of the supply trains made them tempting targets for raiding Comanches, Kiowas, or Apaches. Some of the Mexican officers recognized the transport dangers, and in later years José Enrique de la Peña, referring to Santa Anna's campaign, wrote, "A grave error was made...a strong navy was the primary requirement for this campaign. The main operation of this enterprise should have been by sea."

The Texans agreed it was vital to cut the Mexican sea lines to Texas and force them to make a long enervating march across a hostile land. But how?

Bereft of money, they fell back on an old nautical tradition. In November they issued "letters of marque and reprisal" enabling merchant ships to arm themselves and as legitimate privateers, sweep the seas of Mexican ships.

It was a navy on the cheap, and in effect it was little more than legalized piracy. There were restrictions, however, and the legislation required, at least on paper, that the privateers "should be men of good character."

According to the legislation, the ships should be more than 80 tons and must carry at least "four 12-pound carronades or their equivalent in metal." Only Mexican ships could be attacked, and prizes must be brought into Texas ports. The republic would get twenty percent of the prize money after captured ships and cargo were sold on the open market.

A problem that plagued the Texans, however, was that most of the Mexican foreign trade was carried by American and British merchantmen. Even though they often carried arms and munitions into Mexican ports, when they were seized by privateers or ships of the new republic, the Texans were accused of piracy by both seagoing powers. Seizures of their ships and trials of their seamen followed by apologies from the Texas government were constant problems during the war years.

In addition to the privateers, a committee of the new government represented that "The establishment of a small naval force for the security of our extended coast and the protection of our own commerce is... highly necessary and indispensable...." They recommended "the purchasing, arming and equipping of two schooners of twelve guns, and two schooners of six guns each, to cruise in, and about the bays and harbors of our coast."

Because at that time the Texans were ostensibly fighting for a return to the democratic, liberal Mexican constitution of 1824 that had been usurped by Santa Anna, the committee stipulated that:

The ships "shall carry the flag of the Republic of the United States of Mexico, and shall have the figures 1, 8, 2, 4, ciphered in large Arabics on the white ground thereof."

Privateering commissions were issued to Ira R. Lewis, owner of the schooner *William Robbins*; Robert Potter, who later became secretary of the Texas navy; and three others.

The first privateering commission was awarded to the *William Robbins* to be under the command of the redoubtable Captain William A. Hurd, who had led the *San Felipe* in its bloody victory over the *Correo de Mexico*. Shortly after that victory, however, Hurd ran the *San Felipe* aground in Matagorda Bay while chasing a Mexican vessel and tore out the bottom of that stout ship.

Transferring to his new command, he sailed the *William Robbins* to the site of his wrecked ship, salvaged the *San Felipe* cannon, and mounted them on board his new vessel.

The *William Robbins* was another topsail schooner with two square-rigged sails high on the mainmast, jib sails stretched forward to a long bowsprit, and a large gaff-rigged sail on its mizzenmast. With the *San Felipe* cannon

Chapter 3

added, the seventy-ton schooner mounted six big guns and was manned by a large crew of fifty. A large crew was not unusual for a privateer; although the extra hands made for cramped living, the men provided the necessary sailors to man prize crews. They were also needed as gun crews for the carronades during an engagement while others, from perches on the spars aloft, could use their Texas long rifles to shoot down on enemy crewmen.

On November 19, 1835, Hurd, still in upper Matagorda Bay, received news that a Texas schooner, *Hannah Elizabeth* out of New Orleans, had been driven ashore near Paso Cavallo at the eastern end of Matagorda Island by a Mexican naval vessel. Hurd piped his crew aboard and took with him a contingent of what were now termed "Texas Marines" under the command of Matagorda merchant Samuel Rhoads Fisher. A fearless man, Fisher would later play a major role in the development of the navy of the Republic of Texas.

After a two-day sail fighting head winds, Hurd crossed the bay and landed at the pilot house at the waterway's entrance. There he learned the Mexican warship *Bravo* had put a prize crew aboard the grounded *Hannah* and taken its crew and passengers prisoner. The prize crew had been given orders to place the cargo and passengers in the *Bravo's* longboat, set fire to the *Hannah*, and return to the mother ship.

Their plans were spoiled when a sudden wind gust capsized the longboat, dumping its oarsmen into the water. An incoming tide drifted the boat and its swimming crew onto shore. A few armed and alert Texas militiamen patrolling the area saw the accident and, riding to the scene, took the oarsmen prisoner and seized the boat.

Then, with sudden fierce wind gusts, a Texas "norther" blew into the bay. When the *Bravo* began dragging anchor, its captain hauled it up, and the ship, driven by the wind, was propelled out into the gulf. On the beach the Texans and their prisoners watched forlornly as the Mexican ship's masts receded into the blue.

When the winds moderated, Hurd and twenty marines landed on the sandy spit upon which the *Hannah* was beached. Outnumbered and outgunned, Lieutenant Mateo, commanding the Mexican prize crew, presented his sword to Hurd and surrendered his eleven men.

When Hurd found some of the holds in the *Hannah* empty, he asked its captain, "What happened to the military goods you were carrying?" The skipper replied by pointing over the side of the ship.

"We dumped it overboard when we went aground."

The crew's action was understandable, for the schooner was carrying two 6-pounder and one 4-pounder cannon, 500 muskets, and eighteen kegs of gunpowder destined for Texas military forces. If the Mexicans had found the armaments, it was a sure ticket to facing the sunrise with backs to the wall and staring at the barrels of a firing squad.

The Texans waded into the shallows, located the dumped arms and ammunition, and hauled them up onto the deck of the *William Robbins*. Then Hurd sailed his ship back up Matagorda Bay and landed his cargo, which was a godsend to the ill-equipped Texas military forces.

A sour note to the affair came when the remainder of the *Hannah Elizabeth*'s cargo was sold at auction on the basis of Texas salvage laws. An unpleasant dispute over the sale broke out between Fisher, who had been named agent for the disposition of the cargo, and Colonel James Walker Fannin, who commanded the Texan force at Goliad.

Fannin charged "fraud and corruption" in the auction, and one of his supporters referred to Fisher and Captain Hurd as "bone pickers." The Fannin partisans claimed that

Chapter 3

the "Texas seacoast has produced a scene of fraud, corruption and piracies."

Fisher, a man described as "a most amiable and accomplished gentleman, modest and unassuming," was, nevertheless, not a man to ignore aspersions on his character.

In a sizzling letter to Fannin, he accused the colonel of being "incapable of adhering to the first principles of discretion and truth." Your are, he said, "lost in a sea of defamation and falsehood." Finally, he charged, "Your whining affections of sympathy for the unfortunate belie your Ethiopian speculation and importation of slaves from Africa contrary to the laws of this country."

Fisher concluded his missive with an implied challenge to a duel. Fannin never replied, and his charges became moot a few months later after the hapless colonel was butchered along with his command at Goliad.

Soon after the *Hannah Elizabeth* episode, the *William Robbins*, formerly a privateer ship, was purchased by the new navy department of the Republic of Texas and renamed the *Liberty*. Hurd, given a commission in the Texas navy, was placed in command of the newly purchased schooner-of-war *Brutus*.

Meanwhile, another privateer, the *Terrible*, was living up to its name while commanded by a Lieutenant Randolph. Fitted with brand new guns and a crew who dreamed of becoming rich from the seizure of Mexican ships, it sailed out of New Orleans on November 8, 1835, to raise havoc in the Gulf of Mexico.

It was never determined how many ships and seamen *Terrible* captured, or the nature of their disposal. It was probably just as well, for Lt. Randolph, it would seem, was perhaps more pirate than patriot; albeit, there often was only a thin shade of difference between the two.

Randolph probably sold his "prizes" to crooked dealers in British or French Caribbean ports and thus avoided paying the government of Texas its twenty percent share of the loot.

He was also rather casual about the flags of the ships he was seizing. In a turnabout, after locating her in the Gulf, the United States warship *Boston* sailed up alongside the *Terrible*. The American captain ran out its much heavier cannon and informed Lt. Randolph that he and his ship were under arrest.

Under the *Boston*'s guns, the privateer was sailed into New Orleans where Randolph was charged with piracy for his actions against the Sardinian merchant ship *Pelicana Mexicana*. Randolph probably pled that the ship's name had led him astray. A sympathetic court dropped the charges, and Randolph and the *Terrible* sailed back out into the Gulf to enjoy a few more unrecorded adventures.

Randolph, however, was a bit too much, even for the rambunctious Texan government, and when he returned to Galveston for refitting he was replaced by Captain John M. Allen.

While cruising the coast in the waning days of 1835 and early 1836, Allen helped cripple Mexican efforts to supply Santa Anna's armies by capturing the *Sisal*, *Campeache*, and *Matilda*, all loaded with provisions and ammunition.

After sailing those ships into Galveston harbor, their cargoes kept that beleaguered city from starvation during the disasters that plagued the Texans' hastily assembled armies. For if there was action on the gulf, there was more brutal fighting on the land, and the battles were disasters for Texas arms.

At first things seemed to be going well for the Texans. On November 20 a forage detail sent out by Cos, now in possession of San Antonio, was ambushed and fifty of his

Chapter 3

men killed. On December 20 Texas forces attacked and overwhelmed Cos and captured San Antonio. The Mexican troops, after pledging never again to fight against Texas, were allowed to march south, across the Rio Grande to their base at Monclova.

Santa Anna, now the self-styled "Napoleon of the West," became infuriated at the loss of San Antonio. Determined to crush the Texan revolt, he mobilized a large army at Saltillo and prepared to march on the rebellious settlers.

His second-in-command, General Vicente Filisola, an experienced Italian soldier of fortune, warned against an overland march to the Texan heartland near Galveston. Filisola pointed out that it was 180 miles from Saltillo to the banks of the Rio Grande at Laredo. From there it was 150 miles to San Antonio, the first populous city in Texan territory. Furthermore, to crush the rebellion, Santa Anna would have to march his army an additional 250 miles to Galveston, the commercial hub of Texas.

The march would be across rough, often dry country, offering little forage or water for the expedition's horses, mules, and oxen. In addition to hauling food, ammunition, and cannon, they would have to transport great amounts of water until they reached a major river. They would have to cross the Rio Grande, Nueces, San Antonio, Guadalupe, Colorado, and Brazos Rivers in order to reach the major Texian settlements. There were no bridges, and if they failed to make the river crossings before the spring rains, most of the fords would be flooded. Heavy rains would also wash out the trails, which the Texans laughingly called roads.

Finally, the long animal-hauled logistical tail of the army would constantly be raided at night by bands of Comanche, Kiowa, and Apache warriors. Those fierce brigands would slaver at the opportunity to cut out horses, mules, and wagons from a slow-moving, heavily laden army.

Sensible military doctrine, according to professional Mexican officers, called not for a slow-moving advance over land, but for a swift passage across the Gulf waters to a port on the upper Texas coast. They believed that the Mexican navy should land troops and set up a supply base at Copano Bay, Matagorda, or Brazoria. From there they could move fresh, well-supplied troops into the Texas heartland and destroy the rebellion.

Santa Anna, like Houston, was land-bound in his thinking, and neither appreciated or understood naval strategy or operations. Ignoring advice, he ordered the army to march overland to San Antonio. It was a decision that would cost him the war and Texas.

By mid-February of 1836, after an exhausting march, Santa Anna's forces crossed the Rio Grande and occupied Laredo. With the sea routes threatened by Texas naval forces, Santa Anna made a grim march overland to San Antonio. Because of a shortage of supplies, his troops survived on half rations, but thirst and exhaustion wore down many of his soldiers. Their weakened condition was to have serious consequences later in the campaign.

Although he lost many men and a vast number of draft animals during the trek, Santa Anna believed he had more than enough forces to crush the rebels. He was almost right.

When a fresh "norther" dumped heavy rains on the road to San Antonio, the route became a sea of mud. Reluctantly he abandoned his heavy artillery that became stuck in the quagmire of a road. Impatiently he pushed on with only two batteries of 6-pounder guns.

The Mexican army reached San Antonio on February 23 with four thousand men. There, they found less than two hundred courageous Texans under the command of the

Chapter 3

now Colonel William Barret Travis, Jim Bowie, and Davy Crockett defending a broken down abandoned mission called the Alamo.

William Barret Travis led the Texas settlers in the first revolts against Mexican customs agents. He was later to die heroically defending the Alamo. (Texas State Library and Archives Commission)

The Texans held out for twelve days, but on March 6, 1836, the Mexican army battered their way into the makeshift fort. The defenders fought and died to the last man, and their heroism led to the ferocious battle cry "Remember the Alamo." It was a cry that would haunt Mexican soldiers for the next decade.

On February 17, while Santa Anna was struggling toward San Antonio, General Don José Urrea crossed the Rio Grande at Matamoros with a thousand men. Moving quickly across the flat coastal plain, on February 27 his regulars wiped out a force of fifty Texans at San Patricio and exterminated another small force at Agua Dulce.

By late March Urrea had smashed a Texas contingent under Colonel James Fannin near Goliad and upon Santa Anna's orders shot all 390 helpless prisoners. Later, at a place called San Jacinto, Mexican soldiers would pay a heavy price for their *jefe's* ruthlessness.

General Sam Houston, commanding the last remaining force of the almost annihilated Texan army, was in full retreat. And in what was to be called the "Runaway Scrape," the entire Anglo-Texas population was fleeing eastward as fast as they could go.

Terrified by Santa Anna's atrocities, men, women, and children hitched their wagons and abandoned their homes, farms, crops, and domestic animals in a wild flight toward the Louisiana border.

The government, which had proudly proclaimed Texas independence on March 5, was by March 17 cowering in Galveston along with other frightened refugees from the "Runaway Scrape."

The only large building on the island was a Mexican customhouse, and the refugees were forced to live and sleep on the sand. The lucky ones had salvaged blankets or a canvas awning to shield them from sun, rain, and wind.

Chapter 3

There was fever, near starvation, and hordes of thirsty mosquitoes. The ragged families prayed for a cold north wind to drive away the biting swarms.

Hunger pangs were eased after the *Invincible* captured and looted a Mexican brig loaded with flour and rice. The ship was one of the schooners purchased by the Texas government along with the *Liberty*, *Brutus*, and *Independence*, which constituted the first Texas navy.

The senior captain of the official navy was Charles E. Hawkins, a seagoing adventurer and a former lieutenant in the United States Navy. In 1826 he resigned his commission to join D.D. Porter, a former commodore in the American navy. Porter had left the American service to command the newly formed Mexican navy during its war for independence from Spain.

Hawkins distinguished himself in a battle with the Spanish fleet off the Cuban coast, but with Mexican independence secured he left their navy, returned to the United States, and became employed as a steamboat captain.

In 1835 he was commissioned a major in a Mexican revolutionary force led by José Antonio Mexia. During an attack on Tampico, the insurgents were crushed and Hawkins was one of the few who escaped.

In March 1836 he was appointed captain of the *Independence*. He did yeoman duty on that ship but was unable to engage any Mexican warships. In February 1837, while in New Orleans, he contracted smallpox and died.

The *Liberty*, the old privateer *William Robbins*, now a ship of the regular navy, was put under the command of Captain William S. Brown. She weighed in at a swift sixty tons and carried six cannon and a crew of fifty.

On March 3, 1836, the *Liberty*, some 650 nautical miles from her home port of Galveston, was sailing off the

Yucatan Peninsula near the Mexican port of Sisal when they spotted a large schooner anchored there.

Sailing close in to the port, Brown anchored and ordered two boats lowered. Filled with three dozen armed crewmen and Texas marines, they rowed swiftly toward the ship. On her stern she carried the name *Pelicano*.

The Mexicans were also alert. A lookout spotted the Texan schooner and rang the ship's bell, calling the crew to general quarters to repel boarders. They also sent frantic messages to the port captain appealing for help.

In response twenty soldiers from the Sisal garrison fixed bayonets on their muskets and leaped into rowboats. Both Texans and Mexicans raced to the Mexican ship. Arriving almost simultaneously, the Texans boarded on the seaward side as the Mexicans clambered on board from the port's side, screaming and yelling curses. The two forces met in the middle of the deck. After both sides fired a volley, it was Mexican bayonets against Texan cutlasses and tomahawks.

It was also a study in contrasts. The gaily colored Mexican uniforms contrasted with the sailor garb and rough marine uniforms of the Texans who held a huge height and weight advantage over their smaller opponents. After a furious, hand-to-hand struggle, the Mexican soldiers were all killed and thrown overboard and the *Pelicano*'s crew taken prisoner.

With blood and assorted guts strewn over the decks, the Texans let out a triumphant shout and herded the surviving crew members to the ship's rail. Shouting that they hoped the Mexican sailors could swim, they pushed them over into the harbor waters.

While Captain Brown was prowling through the dark holds checking out the cargo, he noticed barrels labeled harina, manzana, and patala; flour, apples, and potatoes in

Chapter 3

English. Opening them up, however, he discovered muskets and gunpowder.

Putting a prize crew aboard the *Pelicano*, the captured brig and the Texas schooner sailed the more than 600 miles back to Matagorda. Crossing the bar at the entrance to the bay, the heavily laden *Pelicano* ran aground and ripped out part of her bottom.

Quick work by the crews of both ships enabled them to save most of the cargo before the brig sank. The guns and ammunition were added to the dwindling supplies of Sam Houston's army. Houston reported, "The Mexican vessel gave us 420 barrels of flour, 300 kegs of gunpowder and other supplies for the army." One might have thought he would be grateful. He wasn't.

Later, *Liberty*, the smallest of the Texas ships, during an offshore patrol, overran the American-owned brig *Durango*, which was carrying contraband supplies for Santa Anna. After a demonstration of Texan gunfire, she captured the unarmed brig, and a prize crew brought her cargo into Galveston. The capture provided not only a morale boost, but also much-needed supplies to the downhearted Texans.

During the disastrous days of March, the little fleet gave a faint ray of hope to the dispirited families huddling on the Galveston sands. If worse came to worse, they believed the ships could carry them to New Orleans and safety. The fact that there were not enough ships to take them all was a subject they avoided.

To protect against a Mexican sea invasion, the *Invincible* guarded San Luis Pass, the westward entrance into Galveston Bay. The ship, a topsail schooner of 125 tons, was originally built to transport African slaves to the Western Hemisphere. She was built for speed, mainly to evade the British anti-slavery patrols off the African coast. Although lightly framed, she carried an armament of two heavy

18-pounders, two 9-pounders, and four 6-pounder cannon and a crew of seventy.

The *Brutus* under Captain Hurd, termed a "dull sailer," was another topsail schooner of 125 tons, with eight light cannon and a crew of forty. She remained anchored off the eastern end of Galveston Island with her guns trained on the harbor entrance, the one-mile-wide channel between the island and Bolivar Peninsula.

The *Brutus*, a topsail schooner of 125 tons, was commanded by the redoubtable Captain William Hurd. During a cruise in Mexican waters he bombarded the port of Sisal. When he seized the British merchant ship *Eliza Russell* he created an international incident. (Courtesy of the Rosenberg Library, Galveston, Texas)

Chapter 3

The *Independence*, formerly the U.S. revenue cutter *Ingham*, patrolled the Gulf approaches to the Galveston channel. Renamed, she was the same ship that under the command of the tough Captain Ezekiel Jones had, back in June 1835, shot up the *Moctezuma* and threatened to blow up Matamoros. In Texas service she carried one long-range 9-pounder, six 6-pounders, and was manned by a crew of forty.

In addition, the old *Correo de Mexico*, now rebuilt, and a small harbor steamer, the *Cayuga*, constituted the entire Texan navy. But if small in numbers, they were thirsting for action.

The privateer *Flash*, commissioned on March 12, rushed down the coast to the mouth of the Brazos River and sailed up to Velasco. There she found dozens of terrified women and children, refugees of the Runaway Scrape, huddled on the causeway seeking escape from Santa Anna's army. Amid tears and final embraces, the wives and children gathered their few belongings and boarded the *Flash*. As they waved anguished goodbyes, the ship, catching the tide, set sail for Galveston. After watching their loved ones fade into the distance, the men folk shouldered their rifles and marched eastward to join Sam Houston's retreating army.

More importantly, the *Flash* took on board two small cannon, later to be dubbed "The Twin Sisters." They were hauled from Galveston to White Oak Bayou, near a small river called San Jacinto, close to the place where Houston's army was camped. In the ensuing battle they constituted the Texans' entire artillery force.

Meanwhile, Houston had proven to be a reluctant fighter. Under his leadership the undisciplined, untrained, and under-equipped Texas army had known nothing but retreat. For days they had trudged eastward, and as they retreated their friends, neighbors, and relatives were forced to abandon their homes and flee ahead of them.

With each eastward step the volunteers' enthusiasm turned to bitterness. Fleeing women berated them to "stand and fight, you cowards." The volunteers could only grind their teeth in frustration and curse Sam Houston for a coward. Many referred to him as that "God dammed old Cherokee blackguard."

One of the Texan officers, Captain Moseley Baker, humiliated at the retreat, loudly told his men that if Houston did not stand and fight, he would "depose him from command." When news that Colonel James Fannin's surrendered soldiers had been butchered on the orders of Santa Anna, their growing rage knew no bounds.

David G. Burnet, the newly elected provisional president of the Texas Republic, wrote Houston in despair, "Sir: The enemy are laughing you to scorn. You must fight." Soon disgusted volunteers began to leave the army to accompany their fleeing wives and children, and on April 19 the discontent of the troops reached a climax.

The path of the army's retreat came to a crossroads. The left fork led to Nacogdoches and Louisiana; the right led to Harrisburg where Santa Anna was approaching with his army. That morning, during a torrential rain, Captain Baker swore that if Houston rode left, he would depose him by force if necessary.

As the army approached the crossroads, Houston was silent, but the men slogging through the mud started shouting, "To the right boys, to the right." Then the two-man military band of the Texas army, a German fifer and a Negro drummer, without orders, struck up a lively tune, and the army marched to Harrisburg on the way to San Jacinto. Houston followed.

Chapter 3

Santa Anna, flush with victory but short on supplies, had diverted his army from the pursuit of Houston's forces. Instead, he marched his tired troops another 200 miles to Harrisburg in search of both food supplies and the Texas cabinet. They found neither, and an enraged Santa Anna ordered the town burned to the ground. Then, infuriated by the failure of Mexican ships to resupply his men, he camped near Lynch's Ferry. It was close to a small stream called San Jacinto.

Santa Anna's army had suffered many difficulties. Starting from Monclova of February 2, 1836, they had been marching and fighting for more than six weeks. They had slogged through semiarid, barren country where the only vegetation was mesquite, prickly pear, and thin scrub until they reached the Nueces River. There they found rich farmhouses to loot. They appropriated some food and occasionally a few barrels of whiskey to supplement their inadequate rations until they reached San Antonio.

After the debilitating battle at the Alamo, they watched their wounded die for lack of medical attention, then marched on, again short of food. One of Santa Anna's officers, José Enrique de la Peña, described the state of the army as "Pitiful...on half rations...poorly fed...clothed and shod even worse...exposed to hours of burning sun...."

The army was tired, and Santa Anna was careless.

There are two versions of events in the Texan camp as they bivouacked near San Jacinto. One has it that Houston ordered an attack on the Mexican camp. The other is that he ordered a withdrawal, but when his officers forced his hand, he relented, saying, "Attack and be dammed."

Between three and four o'clock on the afternoon of April 21, 1836, the Texans, marching to the music of their band playing "Come to the Bower," attacked the drowsy Mexican encampment.

Legend has it that at the time of the attack Santa Anna was in his tent dallying amorously with a young woman. When he first heard the firing, he dashed from the tent and hid in some swampy ground near the battlefield.

Many of the charging Texans had lost relatives or friends in the massacres at the Alamo and Goliad. In a frenzy of hatred and blood lust, they burst through the enemy lines and slaughtered the dazed Mexican soldiers.

Later in the day, his army destroyed, Santa Anna was captured by a Texan patrol and brought before Sam Houston. While the enraged Texans howled for the dictator's blood, Santa Anna, to save his neck, signed a peace treaty granting Texas full independence from Mexico. Later he would repudiate the treaty and plot to recapture the lost province.

The *Flash*, meanwhile, had landed at Morgan's Point on the mainland. There they found 150 frightened women and children as well as all the remaining members of the Texas cabinet. Somehow they crowded them all aboard and transported them to Galveston Island. Shortly after they landed, news that the Mexican army was heading for Galveston caused a panic, and the entire population was preparing to flee by boat to New Orleans. Their panic was at its height when they heard the joyous report that Houston, on April 21, had destroyed Santa Anna's army and captured the wily Mexican general.

Another Mexican army under the command of General Vincente Filisola, Santa Anna's second in command, was camped near the swollen Brazos River close to the present town of Richmond. Although he was less than forty miles from San Jacinto, Filisola refused to attack the Texas army and ordered a retreat back to the Rio Grande.

Chapter 3

General Antonio Lopez de Santa Anna after losing Texas at San Jacinto lost a leg in a battle with the French. He was reconciled to the loss of the limb but vowed to reconquer Texas. (Texas State Library and Archives Commission)

Of Privateers and Pirates

General Vicente Filisola ordered his army to retreat back to Mexico when he feared Texas warships "Could cut all communications and prevent a supply of provisions" to his half-starved troops. (Texas State Library and Archives Commission)

Although severely criticized by General Urrea for his action, Filisola maintained that, unable to receive supplies by sea, he was forced to put his men on half-rations consisting of hardtack and corn crackers. His troops, he said, were half-starved, sick with dysentery, and low on ammunition. If he fought another battle with the Texans, he believed it would result in a disaster for the Mexican army. He later reported:

"The Texans possessed three steamboats and several schooners situated at Galveston and Matagorda which could make with impunity up-river attacks upon the right flank and rear guard of our troops and place in jeopardy detachments at Copano, Goliad and Matagorda.... They could cut all communications and prevent a supply of provisions."

Filisola's assessment proved true when on June 1 the American-owned schooner *Watchman*, unaware of the Mexican retreat, was attempting to resupply Santa Anna's army. Loaded with provisions, the schooner slipped past the Texan blockade and anchored off the wharf at the small port of Copano (near the present town of Rockport).

While the *Watchman* was waiting for a rendezvous with the Mexican army, unknown to its skipper, a band of Texas horsemen were patrolling in the area. For on May 29, 1836, General Thomas Jefferson Rusk of the Texas army was concerned that Mexican reinforcements and supplies might be brought in through Copano Bay. He ordered Major Isaac Burton, commanding a company of mounted rangers (forerunners of the Texas Rangers) to search the coastal area from Guadalupe to Refugio.

On June 2, after a spy reported the *Watchman* anchored in Copano Bay, Burton's troop made a brisk ride to the area. By 8 o'clock the following morning, after concealing themselves near the water's edge, they signaled the anchored ship by waving a Mexican flag from the beach.

The *Watchman* lowered the ship's longboat, and five sailors rowed to shore expecting welcoming smiles from their Mexican army comrades as they brought needed food and ammunition. The smiles they received, however, were less than friendly, as after they alighted from the boat they looked into the grinning faces and leveled rifles of the Texans.

The sailors were quickly trussed up and led back from the beach while sixteen Texans with Bowie knives and rifles crammed into the boat. Through the haze and the dim morning light, they rowed swiftly to the anchored *Watchman*. Before the ship's company could react, the Texans were over the side and the *Watchman* was theirs.

As the Texans boarded the vessel, the ubiquitous Colonel John Davis Bradburn, now a passenger and slippery as ever, jumped into a small boat alongside the ship. Rowing mightily, he slipped away, again escaping the wrath of the Texans.

Burton scoured the coastal area and finally found enough experienced sailors to sail their prize 125 miles to the northeast to Velasco. But upon attempting to get underway, the lumbering merchantman was unable to make headway against strong northwesterly winds. Frustrated, the *Watchman* dropped anchor and waited for a change in the weather.

Someone in the Mexican crew must have let slip the news that two other Mexican supply ships were scheduled to enter Copano Bay only a few days after the *Watchman*'s arrival.

On this news Burton placed lookouts along the coastal approaches to the bay. They watched and waited for two weeks until one morning they spotted two ships. The

Chapter 3

Comanche and the *Fanny Butler*, flying Mexican colors, were sailing northeast from Corpus Christi Bay. Burton's lookouts tracked them along the route, past Redfish and then Aransas Bay, as they eased past the mud banks littering the waterway. Then they turned north-northwest and entered Copano Bay.

As the two ships came into view, the captain of the *Watchman*, with a gun to his head, signaled their captains to join him for a conference.

Anchoring nearby, the two skippers obligingly had their boats row them to the *Watchman*. As they came aboard, grinning Texans put Bowie knives to their throats, and they were escorted to the ship's cabin and put into irons.

The two boat crews, with pistols pointed at their heads, then rowed details of mounted rangers to their respective ships where the surprised sailors were quickly taken captive.

After the winds shifted favorably, the three ships were sailed to Velasco where their cargos were well received by the Texas forces. As the tale was told all across Texas, Burton and his mounted rangers received the popular title of "The Horse Marines."

The jubilant Texans by now believed the war was over and that Texas was insured peace as a new and independent nation. The jubilation, however, was to be short lived.

CHAPTER 4

Successes and a Failure

It is difficult in the twenty-first century, when worldwide communications travel with the speed of light, to realize the isolation of ships at sea during the 1830s. Dispatches took weeks, sometimes months to arrive with vital information.

While dramatic events were taking place on the Texas mainland, the privateers were raising hell in the Gulf of Mexico even after Santa Anna's surrender. The continuing raids on Mexican shipping were justified, however, when the Mexican government repudiated Santa Anna's treaty of peace with Sam Houston and maintained that Texas was still a subservient province of Mexico. Consequently, the war at sea was to continue unabated.

Refusing to accept or recognize the Texas Republic, the Mexicans planned a reconquest of the breakaway province. And while the Texas army was to rust away from lack of mission, it was Texas ships that frustrated any attempt at a major invasion by Mexican forces.

The impetuous skipper of the armed schooner *Invincible*, Captain Jeremiah Brown, was usually indifferent to

Chapter 4

political events on the mainland. As a seaman, he had a legendary reputation for running schooners and packet boats past Mexican customs stations during the early 1830s.

He was the older brother of Captain William S. Brown, the master of the *Liberty*, and there was a friendly competition between them as to who could ravage the most shipping along the Mexican coast. The brothers' ferocity reached fever peak when they learned that their father, George Brown, had died fighting at the Alamo. William, a resident of Velasco, received most of his early military experience in the army, shouldering a musket during the siege of San Antonio de Bexar in 1835.

He was said to have designed an early Texas flag displaying a bloody arm set on a background of red and white stripes. Underneath the arm was printed the battle cry "Independence." He flew it over Velasco harbor in 1836 and probably flew it from his ship as a battle flag.

During the dark days of March 1836, he was cruising the waters off the Mexican port of Matamoros. On April 3, upon arriving at the mouth of the Rio Grande, a lookout spotted two Mexican ships, the armed schooner *Bravo* and the merchant ship *Correo Segundo*, heading out of port.

While crossing the bar the *Bravo* struck a reef and tore loose her rudder. Twisting helplessly in the ebbing current, she dropped anchor and waited for help. Seeing her condition, Brown hoisted a large American flag from the peak of his gaff.

He dressed young Lieutenant William H. Leving in an American naval uniform and sent him to the Mexican vessel in the ship's boat. After clambering up the *Bravo*'s ladder, Leving gave the Mexican skipper a snappy salute and stated, "The American navy demands an explanation as to why American shipping is being harassed by changes in the port's regulations."

The Mexican captain, who spoke no English, looked blank and turned towards a light-haired officer at his side who translated. The officer was none other that the notorious Thomas "Mexico" Thompson, late of the *Correo de Mexico*. Fortunately he and Leving had never met.

Thompson, released from the New Orleans jail after his piracy charges had been dismissed, had rejoined the Mexican navy and was serving as executive officer on the *Bravo*.

After a brief discussion it was decided to send Thompson aboard the "American navy" ship to coordinate arrangements for making an official protest by the Americans about Matamoros port conditions. But when the Britisher climbed aboard the *Invincible*, there was a shock of recognition when Brown and Thompson eyed each other. The strained moment ended abruptly when Brown ordered the "pirate bastard" put in irons.

The Mexicans, suddenly realizing something was terribly amiss, went to general quarters, but the Texans were quicker. A broadside from the big guns of the *Invincible* spread bloody havoc over the deck of the Mexican ship and silenced her guns.

Suddenly a lookout in the *Invincible*'s crow's nest shouted, "Ship ahoy," as he spotted the topmasts of a large brig flying the Stars and Stripes of an American merchant vessel. Ignoring the *Bravo*, Brown ordered a pursuit of the bigger game. He knew that American ships were carrying war supplies to Mexican ports, and he was determined to get this fat merchantman.

Bending on full sail, the fast schooner soon closed with the big brig. Steering his ship into hailing distance, Brown ran out his guns and demanded the brig to "heave to." Reluctantly the brig, named the *Pocket*, complied. Although the captain protested, Brown led a boarding party onto the brig and demanded to see the ship's papers.

Chapter 4

A pistol pointed at his head dissuaded the brig's captain from further protests, and he handed over the ship's manifests. The papers stated that the *Pocket* was American owned and was sailing out of New Orleans for Matamoros with a cargo of provisions. A search convinced Brown the ship was sailing under false colors.

The Texan captain found dispatches for Santa Anna from spies in Texas and New Orleans that gave military information about Texas troop movements and descriptions of the naval raiders flying the flag of the new republic. Also included "was a chart of the whole coast." It was probably the work of Thompson, and it "minutely laid out" the best locations for landing military supplies. Other dispatches gave instructions for transporting Mexican troops to reinforce Santa Anna's army.

What enraged the Texans most was the presence of three Americans named Somers, Hogan, and Taylor, who were carrying newly minted commissions as lieutenants in the Mexican navy. They were, in the minds of the Texans who were fighting for the life of their country, traitors. Not legally, they conceded, but morally. They were immediately put into irons along with "Mexico" Thompson.

Their treatment was mild compared to the fate of young Lieutenant Leving, who was stranded on the now ignored *Bravo*.

After the *Invincible*'s broadside had blasted the Mexican vessel, the crew took to the boats and abandoned their wrecked ship, taking the Texan officer with them. After they reached shore, Leving was put in irons and thrown into jail. Shortly afterwards he was tried as a pirate before a military court. Early one morning the bewildered young man was taken from his cell, placed against a wall, and shot to death.

En route to Galveston the *Invincible* rendezvoused with the *Brutus* under the command of violent Captain Hurd, formerly the skipper of the privateers *San Felipe* and *William Robbins*. The passengers and crew of the *Pocket* were transferred to the *Brutus*, while a prize crew took over the former Mexican brig. It was not an advantageous transfer for the prisoners. Captain Hurd had them stripped and put into double irons, both hands and feet, and confiscated their personal belongings.

Later Hogan and Lieutenant Don Carlos Ocampo, one of Thompson's former officers, for undisclosed reasons, were brought on deck and tied down over one of the big 18-pounder cannons. A husky mate then proceeded to turn their backs and buttocks into a pulpy mass of bleeding flesh with two dozen lashes each from a cat-o-nine tails. Half dead, they were again placed in irons and thrown back into the hold.

Later, with a hatred that seems almost paranoid, Hurd had all the Americans brought on deck. In sneering tones he announced, "I'm going to hang the lot of you."

The foreyard was loosened and braced, and ropes were attached. Hangman's knots and loops were tied in the loose ends. When a noose was placed around each man's neck, Hurd snarled, "Prepare to die."

As the condemned either prayed or cursed, Hurd let out a raucous laugh. "Put 'em back in irons," he told his quartermaster.

After days at sea *Brutus* sailed into Galveston harbor. While most passengers were transferred to tents on the island, the Americans in the Mexican navy were kept in irons. Somers was kept chained for twenty-five days and Taylor for seven weeks. Finally, after almost half a year of hard labor on the docks, the American prisoners were released and permitted to return to New Orleans.

The *Invincible*, meanwhile, had completed its cruise and delivered the *Pocket* and its cargo to the Texas authorities.

Chapter 4

The capture was hailed as "a most timely assistance to the victors of the field of San Jacinto, who were short of provisions."

By the middle of April, Brown sailed his ship to New Orleans to pick up supplies for the Texas army. If he expected to be treated as a conquering hero, he was sadly mistaken. New Orleans ship owners and merchants had become livid over having their ships and cargoes captured and confiscated by the rampaging Texans.

Their attitude was "To hell with Texas independence, they are seizing our property." The fact that most of it was contraband of war did not concern them. On May 23, 1836, the *New Orleans Bee* newspaper fulminated, "Of what use is the Star Spangled Banner if it can not protect us from the depredations of a petty state creeping into existence."

The Texas agent in New Orleans wrote a frantic dispatch to the authorities in Austin: "We have been compelled to order the *Invincible* back to Galveston; the capture of the brig *Pocket* is considered by the authorities as an act of piracy... information was given me of the intention of the marshal to take the vessel and arrest the crew."

Captain Brown was out of the city on business. Upon learning the city marshal's intentions, the first mate rounded up the crew from New Orleans grog houses and bordellos. Hurriedly hoisting sail, they weighed anchor and sailed out of the port. When they cleared the Mississippi River waters they breathed a sigh of relief, and as they entered the Gulf they began to feel they had made their escape. The hope was shattered when only a few hours later their lookout spied a pursuing sail on the horizon.

Within a short time they were overtaken by the United States Navy sloop-of-war *Warren*. Wisely not choosing to fight the American navy, the *Invincible* heaved to and allowed a prize crew to sail her back to New Orleans.

Arriving there on May 1, 1836, the crew of forty-eight were jailed on charges of piracy. A sympathetic Texan reported that the New Orleans jail resembled the Black Hole of Calcutta and lamented that it was a strange reward for conquering heroes.

After a week in jail, followed by a three-day trial, the court found that no piracy had been committed and released the men, who were then wined and dined as heroes by the people of New Orleans.

The *New Orleans Commercial Bulletin* newspaper eulogized, "We have never seen a finer collection of robust, and honest faced tars, than the prisoners, and in a good cause, we hope they might ever prove invincible."

A few days later the Texas prize crew arrived in port with the *Pocket*, sending the New Orleans owners into another tantrum. After a bevy of lawyers finished arguing the case, Texas agents purchased the vessel to end the controversy.

While the *Invincible* was returning to Galveston, in June 1836, the *Brutus* was anchored in Matagorda Bay when she sighted the Mexican navy brig *Vencendor del Alamo*. The Mexican warship had been dispatched from Veracruz to protect the *Comanche*, *Fanny Butler*, and *Watchman*. She was somewhat late, for arriving off the Texas coast she learned of the capture of those ships by the Texas "Horse Marines."

Severely outgunned, Captain Hurd sent a messenger overland to Galveston to ask for help. When his message arrived, the Texans sprang into action. The light winds of June, however, boded ill for making a fast southerly passage down the curve of the Gulf, but this navy was nothing if not innovative.

The privately owned steamer *Ocean* was put under letters of marque, cotton bales were piled around her decks,

Chapter 4

and volunteer riflemen were welcomed aboard. Then, her paddlewheels churning, she took the *Invincible* and another privateer, the *Union*, in tow. For several days, towlines straining, the steamer chugged down the coast towing the two sailing ships.

When the *Vencendor del Alamo* sighted the Texas flotilla approaching, her captain realized she would be outgunned and out-sailed in light breezes. To avoid participating in a seaborne Alamo, he hoisted every sail in her lockers and got underway for Veracruz.

Cut loose from the steamer, whose fuel supply was by now running low, the *Invincible* pursued in light winds but could not overtake the Mexican ship. For several days the Texas ship patrolled the coast before heading back to Galveston. After taking on provisions and giving the crew a well-earned leave, she returned to the Mexican coast and spent the next two months stifling Mexican commerce as she patrolled the coastline from Matamoros to Tabasco.

The *Liberty*, meanwhile, carried Sam Houston from Galveston to New Orleans for medical treatment for the injury he received to his ankle during the battle of San Jacinto. After delivering Houston, the little tiger of the Texas navy was ignominiously sold to defray expenses of the almost bankrupt Texas Republic. It was a sad ending for a gallant ship and a heroic crew.

In September 1836 both the *Invincible* and the *Brutus*, sea-battered and worn, managed to sail to New York harbor where they underwent an overhaul and complete refit. Not surprisingly, the Texas government was unable to pay the shipyard bills. Both ships were about to be seized and sold at auction when Samuel Swartwout, a wealthy man sympathetic to Texas, paid off the shipyards. Swartwout was a New York financier and business associate of Sam Houston, who had organized a trading post on the Trinity River the previous year. He was a financial partner of Colonel James Morgan, who during the revolution was commandant of Galveston Island. Morgan was later to play a decisive role in Texas naval history

As the *Invincible* was about to leave the harbor, her captain learned of further legal troubles. After departing hastily, he sighted a steamer pursuing him at full speed. He later learned that the boat was carrying arrest warrants charging the *Invincible* and her captain with violating American neutrality laws. Fortunately, a brisk nor'wester blew across the harbor off Governor's Island, and the Texas ship charged out into the Atlantic with a "bone in her teeth."

Although the land battles had ended, the fight for supremacy in the Gulf continued throughout 1836. In October of that year the privateer *Thomas Toby*, named after the Texas agent in New Orleans, put to sea under the command of Captain Nathaniel Hoyt.

Lieutenant William A. Tennison, an officer on the *Toby*, recounted that the ship, formerly a coastal schooner plying between New Orleans and Texas ports, was outfitted with several cannon including a "Long Tom" (probably a long range 18-pounder). It is unknown what flag the privateer flew, although many would have thought the "Jolly Roger" would have been appropriate. By late October the swift schooner plied the Mexican coastal ports of Veracruz, Sisal, Campeche, Matamoras, and Tampico.

On November 10, 1836, Tennison's journal reported they had captured a Mexican schooner and put aboard a prize crew who sailed her to Texas. Then the *Toby* sailed into Tampico harbor and "Played her Long Tom upon the city...not doing much damage except frightening the good people of the town out of their wits."

As the cannonballs began to crash into waterfront buildings, the local militia rushed to the harbor ready to repel

Chapter 4

what they believed was a Texas seaborne invasion. Captain Hoyt was content to send a challenge to any craft in the harbor that dared to come out and fight. When there were no takers, the *Toby* sailed out of the harbor and continued to prowl the coast. In a short time they captured several small vessels and sent them back to Galveston. The *Toby* returned to her home port in the spring of 1837 for supplies and refitting. In May of that year she was off the coast of Yucatan looking for prey.

Cruising near the port of Sisal, the privateer found pay dirt in the form of the large brig *Fenix*. Overtaking the heavily laden vessel, the *Toby*'s Long Tom persuaded her captain to doff her colors and surrender.

A prize crew brought her to Galveston, and the *Telegraph and Register*, a local newspaper, crowed:

"The *Thomas Toby* has just sent into Galveston a very valuable prize, being a large fine brig, strongly built, and capable of being fitted out as a man-of-war, bearing guns heavier than any now in the Mexican Navy. . . . She has on board 200 tons of salt."

Texas port authorities evaluating the ship reported that she had been built recently in Campeche of cedar and ironwood, weighed 274 tons, and was capable of carrying a battery of 12-pounders. She would be, they reported "an excellent addition to the Texas fleet." Nevertheless, the impecunious legislature refused to make the purchase, and it was sold at auction to a Galveston ship owner.

The newspaper in a flight of patriotic fancy wrote, "Fortune favors the brave. It is gratifying that our flag flaunts over one brave band whose dauntless spirits delight to careen with the stormy petrel over the tossing billows where danger lights the path to glory and to fame."

On their next cruise the *Toby*'s dauntless spirits, either brave patriots or greedy pirates, depending on which side you favored, spotted another fat prize in Sisal harbor. The big merchantman *Correo de Campeche* was riding at anchor in the harbor with most of her crew on shore leave when the *Toby* launched two boatloads of Texans armed with cutlass and pistol to board and capture her.

The boats had pulled up alongside the merchantman and the Texans were about to board when a shout from the *Toby* commanded them to return quickly. Yelling through his speaking tube, Captain Hoyt told them a Mexican brig-of-war was racing toward them. At this, the boat crews pulled on their oars with strength borne of desperation until they clambered onto the *Toby*'s decks. Quickly, the privateer weighed anchor and spread all sail.

Then they performed the classic naval maneuver executed when facing what was thought to be a ship with overpowering gunnery. It was called "Sailing the hell out of here."

The *Toby*, like most of her fellow privateers, failed to make any reports of her captures to the Texas government, both to avoid legal complications as well as to deny the new republic its twenty percent of the loot.

An argument over shares of the booty might have been the cause of a mutiny on board the ship in February 1837. For while she was docked in New Orleans, according to fragmentary newspaper reports, the ship's doctor and chief purser were killed in the affray, and the mutineers were thrown into the New Orleans jail.

The last report of the *Toby*'s forays was in the fall of 1837 when the Texas government ordered her to Havana to pick up two brass cannon, which Texas supporters had purchased as a gift to the new republic.

After picking up the cannon, she was returning to Galveston in October 1837 when she was wrecked in a storm while approaching the harbor.

Chapter 4

The depredations of the regular navy and its very irregular privateers had a devastating effect on Mexican military ambitions to retake Texas. In addition, their raids were influential in causing the Yucatan to attempt to break off from the Mexican Republic and declare its independence.

Many Mexican fishing fleets and coastal shippers were located in that southern province, and the failure of the central government to provide protection created bitterness and despair among its merchant chiefs.

The *Diario del Gobierno*, a leading Yucatan newspaper, wrote stingingly on June 18, 1837, that even with the small size and puny armament of the *Toby*, "The evils that a pirate so insignificant as the *Thomas Toby* causes daily to our commerce are very grave."

The newspaper further complained that the Yucatan had strained their economy even more by contributing "Eighty thousand pesos, munitions and sailors to the Mexican navy with no visible results."

But it was not to be an unmitigated string of victories for the Texas seamen. In July 1836 the Texas fleet had blockaded Matamoras for six weeks, stifling commerce there. But by September the *Invincible* and the *Brutus* had withdrawn and were being refitted in New York while the *Liberty* had been sold for nonpayment of debt.

Only the schooner *Independence* was left on patrol, but during the late winter months her skipper, Commander George W. Wheelwright, sailed her to New Orleans for repairs and provisioning.

While there, he took on board Commissioner William Harris Wharton, the Texas Republic's representative to the United States government. Wharton was returning home as a hero after succeeding in securing American recognition of the new republic. In April the *Independence* sailed for her home port of Velasco.

On the morning of April 17, 1837, she was approaching the mouth of the Brazos River. Illness, desertion, and a failure in New Orleans to recruit a competent crew had left her short-handed with a crew of only thirty-one men and boys. Only six of them were experienced seamen. Lieutenant John W. Taylor later commented, "The rest of them did not know one part of the ship from the other." There were not enough hands, both in numbers and experience, to sail the ship and effectively fire her six small 6-pounders and her one long 9-pounder cannon.

At 5:30 that morning her lookout shouted that two tall ships were six miles to windward and bearing down upon her with all sails set. When they came closer they were identified as the Mexican brigs-of-war *Vencedor del Alamo* and *Libertador*.

Commander Wheelwright knew he was in big trouble. Not only was he outnumbered and outgunned by the two big ships, he was also responsible for the safety of Commissioner Wharton.

Vencedor del Alamo had a crew of more than one hundred men and carried six 12-pounders and a long 18-pounder. The *Libertador* under a former British naval officer, D.F.R. Davis, mustered almost 150 men with sixteen big 18-pounder cannon.

To make matters worse, a brisk wind that favored the bigger ships was bearing down from windward. Wheelwright decided to run downwind to Velasco and seek sanctuary up the Brazos River.

Worse still, the sea was running high. With his ship heeled over while racing downwind, water was often sweeping over the decks of the schooner, which had a low freeboard (the height of the deck from the water). The guns of the Texas ship on the lee side (the side of the ship opposite the wind) were consequently often under solid water

Chapter 4

and could not be fired at all. On the windward side, water occasionally poured down the gun muzzles, rendering them useless as the ship "dipped under water."

After a four-hour pursuit, the Mexican ships had closed within range of the 18-pounder chase guns in their bows. Using clever tactics, the *Libertador* sailed within 400 yards of the port bow of the Texan and approached from the weather side. Then she luffed and, turning into the wind, pulled up alongside the *Independence*. At that point she fired a devastating broadside from eight of her big guns.

Shreds of sails, rigging, heavy wooden blocks, and broken spars came crashing down on the Texan deck. Miraculously no one was badly hurt.

The Texans could only reply to the crushing broadsides when, seas permitting, they fired their three smaller 6-pounders and occasionally their long 9-pounder. They were not totally ineffectual, and their larger gun blew away the *Libertador*'s main topgallant sail. Another of their cannon balls struck the gun deck of the *Libertador*, knocking a 12-pounder and its gun crew out of commission. Still another solid shot chipped a mast, hurling lethal splinters across the deck, tearing down rigging, and killing two of the Mexican crew.

Some surcease from the pounding resulted when the *Libertador*, turning to windward in order to fire her broadside, fell behind the Texas ship. The *Vencedor del Alamo*, however, continued to sail in the wake of the *Independence* and kept up a running fire with her big chase guns. Fortunately, the high seas made for poor marksmanship.

As the *Independence* sailed within viewing distance of the harbor at Velasco, there was hope she might escape. The booming of the guns had been heard in the Texas port, and all of her citizens were gathered on shore or on the causeway watching the battle with growing anxiety.

Successes and a Failure

By 11 o'clock that morning, the wind stiffened. The *Libertador* gained ground, pulled abeam of the Texan ship, and fired another full broadside while *Vencedor* crept up astern.

That broadside let loose a hail of solid shot plus a rain of grape shot and canister. The blast raked the stern of the *Independence*, and grape shot struck Wheelwright as he stood on the quarterdeck shouting orders through a large brass speaking trumpet. The shot slammed the trumpet from his hands and mangled three of his fingers. Another shot struck him in the right side. Bleeding badly, he was carried below. Groaning, he ordered Lieutenant John W. Taylor to take command of the ship.

With her sails sliced by cannon balls, rigging slashed, and the hull perforated, the *Independence* staggered as the two Mexican brigs closed in for the kill.

By 11:45 that morning, *Vencedor* was close on the weather quarter of the Texan ship ready to fire another devastating broadside. The *Libertador*, abeam on the lee side, sailed within fifty yards range, ready to rake with solid shot and canister from her big guns and musket balls fired by the crewmen lining her deck.

Realizing the situation was hopeless and wishing to prevent his young sailors from being slaughtered, Wheelwright ordered Lt. Taylor to haul down the Texas flag and surrender the ship. It was to be the only time in the history of the Texas navy that a ship was surrendered in combat.

When the Texas colors were struck, the hapless spectators on shore let out an audible groan. But all things considered, the *Independence* had put up a gallant fight.

The victorious Captain Davis instructed Lt. Taylor to come aboard the *Libertador* to formalize the surrender. After he boarded the Mexican ship, the young lieutenant, shaken but defiant, faced the British captain serving in the

Chapter 4

Mexican navy. Proudly he stated, "I surrender my ship, but I shall never surrender my sword." With that, he strode to the rail, drew his sword from its scabbard, and with an oath, broke it over his knee and hurled the shattered pieces over the rail into the water.

"Sir," he said, "I am now your prisoner."

The schooner *Independence*, outnumbered and outgunned by two Mexican brigs of war, was battered into surrender in a battle off the mouth of the Brazos River. She was the only Texas ship ever defeated in battle. (The University of Texas Institute of Texan Cultures at San Antonio)

Captain Davis and the Mexican Commodore Lopez were souls of gallantry to the defeated Texans and reassured them they would be treated as honorable prisoners of war. After the slaughters of the Alamo and Goliad, this was welcome news. With the *Independence* in tow, the ships sailed to the Mexican port of Brazos Santiago where Ambassador

Wharton and the officers and crew were lodged in the port's jail.

The Mexican authorities were jubilant at the capture of Wharton, who was not only a close friend and confident of Stephen F. Austin but had also been a leader in the movement for Texas independence. When hearing the news of the capture, John Austin Wharton, the younger brother of the commissioner, requested that Houston put pressure on the Mexican government to extend diplomatic immunity to his brother and release him from prison. His request was all but ignored.

John Wharton, a former officer on Houston's staff and a veteran of San Jacinto, was not to be put off by Houston's seeming inaction and indifference to the fate of his brother. When diplomacy failed, the younger Wharton chartered the schooner *Orleans* and put on board thirty Mexican soldiers who had been captured at San Jacinto. Then he set sail for Matamoros hoping to negotiate an exchange of prisoners.

On October 2 he anchored off the port of Matamoros and hoisted a white flag. When the *Orleans* was boarded by a Mexican customs boat, he handed its officer a letter to the port commander requesting permission to land. He would, he wrote, immediately set his prisoners free and then negotiate for the release of the Texans.

That night, while waiting for the port commander's reply, one of the Gulf's terrible autumn storms blew up and struck the anchored *Orleans*. The screeching winds whipped the waters at the mouth of the Rio Grande into a raging frenzy. The *Orleans*, swinging wildly on her anchor lines, soon sprang leaks, and seawater began to pour into the hull.

The terrified Mexican prisoners were quickly untied and set free. Clambering up from the flooding hull to the deck, some of the men were put to work on the ship's pumps

Chapter 4

while others formed a bucket brigade. Texans and Mexicans alike worked side by side to save the battered ship. The water, however, was pouring in faster than they could pump or bail it out.

Then the straining anchor lines finally snapped, and the *Orleans*, beyond control, was driven toward shore. A surging onshore current, driven by the storm, propelled the ship south of the river's mouth until it smashed onto a sandbar. As the waves hammered the ship's hull into rubble, those aboard grabbed floating debris or struggled onto the bar, fighting to keep their heads above water.

Throughout a terrifying night they fought for their lives. With the dawn the storm vanished as quickly as it came. Although exhausted, the Texans and their former prisoners cheered wildly when Mexican boats arrived to take them safely ashore. Miraculously, only two men drowned.

When the survivors landed on the Matamoros docks, the former prisoners were cheered by a waterfront crowd. The Texans were thrown into jail.

The only good news was that John learned of brother William's escape. It must have been both an ironic and odious surprise to the younger brother when he was tossed into the same cell block in which his older brother had been lodged.

There he learned that shortly before William launched his rescue attempt, an Irish priest, one Father Muldoon, smuggled clerical garb into Ambassador Wharton's cell. After significant funds were exchanged, the Texas diplomat, wearing a turned around collar and a pious smile, accompanied by his Irish benefactor, walked past the guards and out of the prison into a dark night. Parting with the priest, Wharton trekked across the desolate landscape until he reached the Rio Grande. Then it was only a short swim across the muddy river to safety and freedom.

Successes and a Failure

The first Texas Minister to the United States, William H. Wharton was taken prisoner when the *Independence* was forced to surrender. Later, he made a daring escape from a Mexican prison and returned safely to Texas. (Texas State Library and Archives Commission)

Fortunately, a few weeks later the ubiquitous Father Muldoon arrived at John's cell and repeated his performance. Bribing the guards, he led John and a few of his crew out the prison doors and guided them to the river and safety.

By the end of October the two brothers were reunited at the port of Velasco. A residue of their imprisonments was a mutual hatred for Sam Houston, whom they believed had not raised a finger to help them.

Some time after John's escape, an interesting surprise awaited the still imprisoned Captain Wheelwright. The first visitor to their cells was the infamous Captian "Mexico" Thompson, who seemed to be always drifting through the affairs of the Texas navy.

Thompson, who had been given command of the new sloop-of-war *Bravo*, greeted the recovering Wheelwright and his crew warmly. According to Lt. Taylor, he "extended every civility and kindness." And after the Britisher's rather ghastly treatment as a prisoner under the demonic Captain Hurd, his generosity was welcome, if surprising.

During July, when it appeared that an exchange of prisoners between Texas and Mexico had failed, Thompson conspired with Wheelwright and the *Independence* ship's doctor to escape. How he managed it is lost to history, but Mexico in those days was not immune to corruption. Most likely, one dark night a large sum of pesos changed hands, a cell door was left unlocked, and two prisoners and a British captain eased through the jail doors, slunk down to the waterfront, and boarded a small sloop.

Then, silently weighing anchor, hoisting sail, and bidding a quiet *adios* to their captors, they sailed out into the darkness, heading north.

Thompson's motive in arranging the escape is not known. He never disclosed whether he had a falling out with Mexican authorities or was bored with constantly speaking Spanish. More likely he decided his financial advancement would be better gained in Texas. A man of many idiosyncrasies, he may have taken the risk on a whim or just for the hell of it.

After shepherding the Texans home, he was rewarded by a grateful republic by receiving a commission as postcaptain in the Texas navy and was put in charge of the navy yard at Galveston.

In October, after the Texas Congress passed a resolution authorizing reprisals upon Mexican citizens, the remainder of the crews of the *Independence* and the *Orleans* were set free and returned to Texas. When they arrived in Galveston in November, the Congress withdrew the resolution.

Chapter 5

Sweeping the Mexican Main

Although Santa Anna had signed a treaty granting the independence of Texas, the Mexican government was not prepared to let the province go without another fight. During the winter of 1836, General Nicolas Bravo concentrated a large army at Matamoros. Bravo boasted that soon he would overwhelm the Texas army and recapture Texas for Mexico.

The Mexican Minister of War, General Don Jose Maria Tornel, however, cancelled Bravo's attack plans. The political situation in Mexico was explosive, and Tornel realized there were other potential rebellions festering in many provinces. It was wise, the minister believed, to keep the troops at home. Frustrated at abandoning a land campaign, Tornel turned to the sea.

By the spring of 1837 the balance of power in the Gulf of Mexico was swinging back in favor of a reconstituted Mexican navy. In April the Mexican government announced a blockade of Texas ports, and by the middle of the month they positioned three brigs-of-war and two armed schooners on patrol off Galveston. Soon they began seizing ships

Chapter 5

bringing food supplies to the half-starved Texas garrison there.

Many of the captured ships were American owned, sailing out of New Orleans. American naval authorities objected that these seizures violated a Treaty of Amity and Commerce signed by the United States and Mexico and that the ships, under law, should be released by the Mexican navy.

Commander William Mervine of the United States navy's 18-gun sloop-of-war *Natchez* arrived off Matamoros in April at the request of the American consul there. Mervine was a forty-six-year-old veteran of the War of 1812 during which he was wounded in one of the battles on Lake Erie. He was a fiery commander who was not loath to fight if he believed American rights were being trampled.

He contested the legality of the Mexican brig-of-war *General Urrea* capturing the American merchantman *Louisiana* and bringing her into Matamoros to be sold as a prize. Under the treaty of Amity and Commerce, the Mexicans were required to first warn a ship to leave the Texas coast if they suspected it was carrying contraband. The law also stated they could only seize a vessel after a further violation of the blockade.

Under the circumstances, Mervine requested that the Mexican captain release the *Louisiana*. Upon his refusal, Mervine sent a boatload of marines and a prize crew into the harbor. The Americans boarded the *Louisiana*, released the crew from the brig at bayonet point, and sent the Mexicans ashore. The restored captain and crew set sail for the Texas coast, convoyed by the *Natchez*.

Returning to the mouth of the Rio Grande, Mervine was aware that another American ship, the *Champion*, had been seized and held in Matamoros.

Anchored outside the bar, the big Mexican brig *General Urrea* was riding at its mooring. Although the Mexican ship outgunned him, Mervine anchored close to the big Mexican and opened up his gun ports. Then he sent a letter to the captain of the port stating he wanted the *Champion* and its crew freed immediately.

He would, he said, hold the Mexican ship of war hostage to the release of the American ship. Mervine informed the captain of the *General Urrea* that if he hauled anchor, he would be blown to hell. It was called, in those days, a Mexican standoff.

Meanwhile, as gunners in both the United States sloop-of-war and the Mexican brig-of-war eyed each other warily across a few hundred yards of water, more actors entered the scene.

The Mexican gun brig *General Teran* had captured two American merchantmen, the *Julius Caesar* and the *Climax*, off the coast of Texas. After putting prize crews aboard them, all three vessels sailed for Matamoros. Flush with triumph, the trio of ships suddenly appeared off the harbor.

Sighting the *Natchez*, whose skipper had a reputation for ferocity, the Mexican commander reversed his course and turned southeast toward a more friendly port on the lower coast.

Mervine then faced a dilemma. If he pursued the "unholy" trio, the *General Urrea* would escape. If he continued to hold the *Urrea* under his guns, two illegally seized American ships and their crews would be whisked away and possibly never recovered. He resolved the problem by sending a boarding party of Marines with fixed bayonets to the *Urrea* demanding surrender.

The captain of the Mexican ship, determined to preserve his tenuous honor, viewed the hard-faced United States Marines and the poised cannon of the *Natchez* and

Chapter 5

propositioned the boarding party. He told them that if the *Natchez* would fire a cannon shot at him, then bowing to superior force he would surrender.

It seemed reasonable to Mervine, and he ordered a cannon ball fired across the *Urrea*'s bow. As the ball splashed into the water, the Mexican brig lowered its colors in submission. A *Natchez* prize crew boarded the vessel, and the Mexican crew were allowed to row ashore in the ship's boat.

With everyone's honor now secure, Mervine hauled anchor and under full sail set off in pursuit of the *General Teran* and its two captures. Something like a Keystone Kops chase now ensued as the three Mexican ships spotted their pursuers. As the four sailing ships maneuvered in quirky winds, the Mexican commander again reversed his course. Doubling back, he tried to slip his ships past the American and run them into the safety of the port of Matamoros.

The *Julius Caesar* made it. The *Climax* was cut off and surrendered to a *Natchez* boarding party. The brig *General Teran*, fleeing frantically, ran aground on the bar.

By this time Mexican harbor defense forces had manned artillery batteries along the port entrance. As Mervine boldly entered the port to recapture the *Julius Caesar*, he was bombarded on three fronts.

General Teran, still stuck on the bar, opened fire; *General Bravo*, anchored in the harbor, joined in the bombardment; and the shore batteries blasted away at the impetuous Yankee sloop-of-war.

This was a bit too much of a challenge even for Mervine, and although the Mexican gunnery was ineffective, he hauled to the wind and sailed out of the harbor.

Declaring the Mexican blockade of the Texas coast a farce and only a "paper" declaration, Mervine cruised northeast along the Texas coast without sighting any Mexican ships of war.

Perhaps he reflected that, although a neutral, he had done a first-rate job of temporarily wrecking Mexican sea power in the Gulf. In a space of a few weeks he had chased the *General Teran* aground, blockaded the *General Bravo* in port, shelled Mexican shore batteries, freed the American vessels *Louisiana* and *Climax*, and shamefully, in the opinion of the Mexican government, captured the brig-of-war *General Urrea* and sailed it to Pensacola as a prize.

In effect, he had destroyed the Mexican blockade of Texas and restored the commerce that kept the infant republic alive. American ships again sailed freely into Texas ports. Whether by design or happenstance, an American naval officer had provided a great Texas naval victory.

If he had helped Texas, he did little to hurt his career, although he was court-martialed for his belligerent actions in the Gulf, and the *General Urrea* was returned to Mexican authorities with profound apologies. In later years, following brilliant service in the war with Mexico, Mervine was promoted to rear admiral and retired with great honors in 1862.

The return of the *General Urrea* and the American apology was not enough to assuage Mexican anger. Their minister of war, complaining that the gringos had broken their blockade, railed:

"All nations have respected this inherent right of sovereignty of our country except the United States, who escort all ships going to the Texas Coast with their fleet. This enables such vessels to carry contraband of war such as arms, munitions and volunteers for our Texas enemies."

In April the Texas navy was back in action. The *Brutus* and *Invincible*, returning from their refitting in New York, had arrived in Galveston thirsting for action.

Chapter 5

The land-locked mind of Sam Houston, now the elected president of the new republic, was to become the main obstacle to achieving naval supremacy in the Gulf. While he was a leader of some virtues, Houston was totally ignorant of the strategic role the Texas ships played in the successful rebellion against Mexico. The navy, he believed, was an unnecessary expense for a bankrupt republic.

Peeved at the New York shipyard expenses run up by Captain Hurd of the *Brutus* and Captain Brown of the *Invincible*, Houston ordered that the captains be summarily relieved of command upon their ships' arrival at Galveston. To paraphrase the words of the Napoleonic foreign minister Charles Maurice de Tallyrand, "This was not only criminal treatment; it was a grave mistake." With Captain Wheelwright captured and Hurd and Brown fired, Texas had lost its three most experienced naval officers.

Following the *Hannah Elizabeth* imbroglio, Samuel Rhoads Fisher was elected to the Texas Independence Convention and became a signer of the Texas Declaration of Independence. On October 26, 1836, Houston appointed him Secretary of the Navy of the Republic of Texas. From his years as an owner of a shipping business, Fisher understood the strategic necessity of protecting the trade routes to the new republic.

He understood that the new navy must be able to sweep Mexican commerce raiders from the Gulf of Mexico or the economy of Texas would be destroyed. Time, he realized, was running out, and it was vital to send the remaining two Texas ships out to sea. For even after Mervine's depredations, the Mexicans were soon able to put eight men-of-war into a renewed blockade of Texas ports, again posing a threat to strangle commerce.

Samuel Rhoads Fisher, a former fighting Texas Marine, while secretary of the Texas navy defied the orders of Sam Houston and sailed on a successful campaign against Mexican shipping. (The University of Texas Institute of Texan Cultures at San Antonio)

In consultation with Commodore Henry L. Thompson, the new skipper of the *Invincible*, Fisher approved a risky strategy.

Chapter 5

He realized that if the two remaining Texas warships stayed in port, they would be blockaded by a superior force and rendered useless. The Mexican Gulf squadron would then be free to destroy or capture any ship approaching or leaving a Texas port.

The alternative, he decided, was to have the *Brutus* and the *Invincible* slip out to sea and raid the Mexican coast, shooting up ports and capturing merchantmen. This, they believed, would force the enemy fleet to leave the Texas coast to pursue and destroy the raiders. Sound though the plan was, it was refused by Houston, who wanted the ships to remain in Texas waters.

Thus began another in a series of rancorous disputes between Houston and those who understood maritime strategy. Some knowledge of the geography of Mexican waters was necessary to understand the plans of Fisher and Thompson. Houston either lacked that knowledge or failed to understand it.

The northwestern coast of the Gulf of Mexico from New Orleans to Matamoros is crescent shaped. From Matamoros the Gulf curves in a southerly direction until it reaches Coatzacoalcos in the state of Veracruz. From there it swings into a northeastern curve until it reaches the Yucatan port of Sisal, some 700 miles south southeast of Galveston. Overall, from New Orleans to Sisal the Gulf coastline resembles a large letter C. It is shorter and much easier to sail across it, rather then march around it.

The eastern coastline of Mexico, like that of Texas, offers few deepwater ports to the mariner. Most shipping out of New York, New Orleans, or from European ports was destined for Veracruz. Other secondary ports were Matamoros and Tampico. The remainder of Mexico's east coast harbors were mostly used by fishing boats and small coasters.

Mexico, like Texas, had very limited industrial production, and it was necessary to import most of the manufactured goods vital to their economy. Consequently, they were vulnerable to both the blockade of their ports and attacks on their merchant ships.

Fisher and Thompson believed that their swift-sailing armed schooners could raise havoc with Mexican shipping and thereby strangle their economy. The Mexican coastline from Matamoros to the eastern tip of the Yucatan stretched more than 1,200 miles. Furthermore, their major ports were hundreds of miles apart.

The Mexican navy, they believed, although superior to the Texan ships, lacked the strength to effectively patrol this massive coastline.

Houston's preferred course of action, which was to keep the *Brutus* and the *Invincible* in a purely defensive posture in Texas waters, was an idea born of stupidity. If the two Texans fought the eight big enemy ships, some of which were captained by hired, experienced British naval officers, they would undoubtedly be destroyed.

The only solution to Houston's ignorance and intransigence, Fisher decided, was insubordination. Houston would call it mutiny and treason.

On June 10, 1837, Thompson on the *Invincible* and Captain James D. Boylan, the new skipper of the *Brutus*, convoyed the merchant ship *Texas* carrying munitions and food supplies to the Texas detachment on Matagorda Island. The next day, Boylan later reported, they set sail for the "mouth of the Mississippi in hopes to fall in with some Mexican vessels." In the absence of prey, after a few days they sailed for the Mexican coast in defiance of their president's orders.

A passenger on the *Invincible* was none other than Secretary of the Navy Fisher. Whether the secretary joined the

Chapter 5

cruise seeking adventure and sea battles or to escape the wrath of a choleric Sam Houston, he didn't say. Probably both.

In concert, the two ships maintained a southerly course toward the Yucatan peninsula. On July 1, after a consultation at sea, they decided to make Isla Mujeres, located off the northeast coast of the peninsula, a point of rendezvous.

Isla Mujeres (Island of the Women) was a Caribbean paradise with white sand beaches, clear lagoons, and coral reefs. Located a few miles off the eastern tip of the Yucatan peninsula, it was named after statues of Mayan goddesses found there. More important to the Texans was that it provided a sheltered anchorage between the west side of the island and the mainland.

Boylan took the *Brutus* to the western coast of Cuba, hoping to capture Mexican vessels trading in the area. Not finding a prize worth taking, after a few days he took a heading for Isla Mujeres, rounding the Yucatan's Cape Catoche and reaching the island on July 8.

On reaching the island, Boylan found the *Invincible*, which had preceded him by a few days. Thompson had captured and stripped a number of local small canoes, rigged with fore and aft sails, which were called pirogues. One of the largest was loaded with a cargo of logs.

Thompson, a skipper who was part patriot, part entrepreneur, and probably part pirate, having no use for the cargo, sold it back to the owners for $600. Then he split the proceeds with his crew of like mien. It was a policy that would cause him considerable trouble later on.

Needing fresh water and food supplies, the Texans sent small boats ashore to the small villages and scattered islands off the northeast coast of the Yucatan. There they found the water they needed and an additional supply of food in the turtles caught by the islanders.

On July 13 they went ashore on the beautiful island of Cozumel and like thousands of American tourists of the twentieth century, considered it the closest thing to paradise on earth.

Cozumel, located about fifty miles south of Mujeres, is a large island almost thirty miles long and ten miles wide. It is situated twelve miles off the mainland. It boasts marvelous beaches of glittering white sand. Beyond the beaches the island was filled with fruit trees and maize (Indian corn) fields. More important, it provided delicious fresh water and its lagoons were filled with turtles and fish.

Commodore Thompson, enraptured by the island, wrote, in the best spirit of "Manifest Destiny," that Texas must annex this paradise. It would be, he said, "one of the greatest acquisitions to our beloved country that the Admiral aloft [presumably he meant God, who must surely be on the side of the Texans] could have bestowed on us."

Bringing his crews ashore, except for the gunners, Thompson had them construct a forty-five-foot flagpole. With all of the Texans plus a large group of amiable if rather confused islanders assembled, he had the Texas flag run up the flagpole. He then declared the island of Cozumel to be in the sole possession of the Republic of Texas.

The declaration was followed by a twenty-three-gun salute by the two Texas warships, which, if nothing else, scared the hell out of the bewildered islanders.

CHAPTER 6

Charging Lancers and a Castle

The Texas flotilla left Cozumel on July 16, 1837, loaded with casks of fresh water and a large supply of turtles. They rounded Cape Catoche and headed northwest, searching for prey. On July 22 they roamed past the port of Sisal on the northwest corner of the peninsula and spotted the schooner *Union* anchored in the harbor. Thompson sent a boarding party into the harbor, and they quickly captured the ship and its surprised crew. When a few alerted Mexicans on shore shot at them, the Texans responded by shelling the town for three hours.

Combing the coast, they sent boarding parties to many of the coastal towns, foraging for food and fresh water, rarely finding any resistance from the local Mayans.

It was different when a landing party hit the beach at the small fishing village of Chilbona on July 24. The party was led by Captain Boylan accompanied by Secretary Fisher and six sailors. After they beached their longboat and marched about one hundred yards toward the town, they got the surprise that nearly ended their lives.

Charging out from behind some sand hills came a detachment of irregular Mexican cavalry at the gallop. The Texans stared wide-eyed at the frothing horses and the gimlet-eyed riders. They wore huge sombreros and were armed with twelve-foot lances with bright red pennons fluttering from shiny steel spearheads. Other riders waved long swords or cutlasses while some fired a volley from *escopetas* (Mexican shotguns). The Texans froze for a second, then they made a panic run back to the boat.

As the sailors gave mighty heaves to break their longboat loose from the soft sand of the beach, Fisher, armed only with a pistol, turned and fired at the oncoming horde. The secretary, presumably having more than his fill of seagoing adventure for the day, aimed true and blew one of the riders out of his saddle. Then he turned and scrambled into the boat with the rest of the shore party.

Rowing frantically, the oarsmen managed to get beyond pistol and shotgun range. Cursing and waving their weapons in frustration, the horsemen rode out into the surf but soon had to turn back. Just as the Texans breathed a sigh of relief, another detachment of soldiers brought up two small cannon onto the beach and opened fire.

Their shooting was inaccurate, and Boylan remarked their shots "didn't come within twenty yards of us." Commodore Thompson, however, was unforgiving of the Mexican attack.

In his report to the Navy Department upon his return to Galveston on August 29, he admitted:

"Previous to this attack we had acted with every degree of humanity toward our enemy, but from that time our feelings became excited and I gave an order to this effect—To burn, sink and destroy every thing we came athwart. Then we commenced burning their towns, names which at present I cannot remember."

Chapter 6

According to a story in a Galveston newspaper, which later recounted the exploits of the flotilla, Thompson was so enraged that he burned eight coastal towns to the ground. His pique, however, was a mistake, as only a few years later Yucatan would become an ally of Texas as both waged a war of independence with Mexico.

Having vented his spleen, Thompson ordered Boylan to send a ship's boat on a reconnoitering mission along the coast. Standing out to sea in the daylight, when night fell the crew rowed toward shore and with muffled oars silently slipped along the shoreline searching for seagoing victim ships.

Boylan began to worry after they were gone for two days, but on the evening of the third day the scouting party returned, having spied two Mexican schooners, the *Adventure* and the *Telegrafo*, in the harbor at Sisal.

On July 26 the two Texas ships sailed into Sisal, and Thompson dispatched boarding parties who captured both anchored ships. Then Thompson put one of the Mexican prisoners on a canoe with instructions to deliver a note to the local *jefe*. With what might be called a lack of subtle diplomatic language, the note brazenly stated:

"I have sufficient force to take your town. I request you remove to some place of safety the women, the children and old and decrepit persons, as I intend bombarding the town, unless you pay the government of Texas the small sum of $25,000, in consideration of which I guarantee immunity from molestation for six months."

Sir Henry Morgan couldn't have phrased it more succinctly.

When no answer was returned at dawn July 27, Boylan later wrote, the Texan ships "sailed close-hauled into the town with a flag of truce flying." Then at 7 o'clock that morning the Mexican response became obvious when a castle at the south end of the small bay opened fire on them.

Thompson complained, "Their reply was a 24-pound shot close under our main chains while our white flag was still flying at the fore. This want of respect to our flag of truce induced me to open our broadside on the town and castle."

Unfortunately for the Texans, the quality of their gunpowder was bad and their shots fell harmlessly in the water short of the castle. After the shooting started, Thompson ordered the flags of truce hauled down. To the beat of their ships' drummers, the Texans hoisted the flag of the Lone Star Republic to the topmasts of their vessels.

During the early morning the wind died completely and both ships rocked in the still waters. But Thompson was not to be thwarted. "Boats away," he commanded. The ships' gigs and longboats were lowered into the water, lines were attached to the mother ships, and with only the muscle power of the rowers the Texas flotilla went into battle.

Mexican cannon balls whizzed over their heads or soaked them with saltwater as some of the projectiles splashed into the water near them. The oarsmen towed the ships within close range of the waterfront as leadsmen in the bows shouted out water depth. Finally, when there was only thirteen feet under their hulls, the boat crews rested their oars.

Thompson, who had eased his ship closer to the shore than *Brutus*, ordered both ships to drop anchors with spring lines on their cables.

By making the lines fast to the anchor end of their hawsers and leading the lines aft, they could cover all points of the compass with their guns. Heaving in on the lines while slacking the hawsers, the ships could be veered or backed with respect to the anchors. In this manner the Texas ships

Chapter 6

could bring the main guns on either side to bear on their targets.

With the castle bearing south-southwest, *Brutus* opened fire with their starboard broadside and the pivot gun located amidships. The *Invincible* then opened up a "heavy and incessant" fire on the town.

The Texans, for all their boldness, however, had entered a hornet's nest. The castle to the south, flanked by a "round fort" from the northern end of the harbor and a "large gun" on the beach near the harbor mole, began to blast at the anchored Texans.

Thompson estimated the castle mounted six big guns ranging from 18- to 32-pounders in addition to other artillery planted behind bushes on shore. "We stood them a fight of two hours and forty minutes," he reported. Miraculously, no serious damage was done to the ships, but Thompson maintained "few of our shots were wasted."

But under the continuing rain of Mexican shot, he realized it was only a matter of time until they would be hit badly. He later wrote:

"Finding all that we had to lose and but little to gain as we had more than one thousand men to contend with, we thought it most prudent to shift our quarters further out."

In other words, they got the hell out of there.

Later, Thompson complained, "The hot shot which we fired was merely cold shot warmed and did not have the desired effect or we could have burned the whole town which consisted of about one hundred houses."

If Thompson was furious about the state of his munitions, he took out his wrath on his crew. No Nelson he, a calm demeanor during combat was not his style. He stalked his quarterdeck in a wild fury, and when an *Invincible* cannonball missed its mark, he loudly remarked on the undoubted canine ancestry of the gun crew.

For some failure, real or imagined, in the middle of the fight, he ordered his bosun's mate arrested and clapped into irons. His screaming "Goddamms" worried some of the more pious, or more superstitious, members of the crew who feared he would bring down upon them the wrath of the Deity.

After the flotilla reached the safety of Gulf waters, Boylan reported, "On this day every officer and man on board did his duty undauntedly and cheerfully."

The newfound cheer among the motley crews was probably the result of Thompson ransoming the *Union* and its cargo from the owners and paying out the then large sum of $527.37 to each member of the crew. This, of course, was highly illegal as under law, Thompson was required to return the ship and its cargo as a prize to a Texas court where its value would be adjudicated by a maritime commission.

It did, however, take much of the sting out of the commodore's fulminations.

Following a council of war, Thompson ordered the *Adventure* burned as "She was a dull sailor." He ordered forty captured Mexican sailors into boats and landed them ashore. Then the *Brutus, Invincible,* and the *Telegrafo* headed north for a sixty-mile passage to the Alacranes Islands.

They dropped anchor there on July 31. Thompson assigned a prize crew to the *Telegrafo* and dispatched it to Texas for sale. While *Brutus* engaged in a futile chase of a swift Mexican schooner, *Invincible* captured the 80-ton schooner *Albispa* with a cargo of crockery and hardware.

On August 3 the luck of the *Brutus* turned for the better. Early in the morning a lookout espied a sail to windward. Boylan had all sails hoisted and gave chase. By 10 o'clock

Chapter 6

he caught her and, sailing alongside, opened his gun ports and signaled her to heave to.

A boarding party found her to be the 180-ton schooner *Eliza Russell* out of Liverpool and bound for Sisal with a full cargo of various goods. Boylan had her sailed to the Alacranes where Thompson judged her cargo to be contraband and ordered a prize crew to sail her back to Galveston. There was a scent of piracy in this seizure, and it would rebound on both Boylan and Thompson at a later date.

On August 6 Boylan went ashore on one of the main islands of the Alacranes and, not to be outdone by his commanding officer, had his men raise a flagpole and hoisted the Lone Star flag. Then with pomp and solemnity, he annexed the islands in the name of the Texas Republic.

Although anchoring on the lee side of the island provided some small protection from the blows of a sudden norther, it was hardly a prize possession.

The Islas Alacranes consisted of five small coral atolls some seventy-eight miles north of the Yucatan port of Progreso. There is no fresh water on the islands, rainfall is scarce, and the sandy soil contains little vegetation. The half dozen itinerant fishermen and hundreds of sea birds witnessing the ceremony must have wondered at the strange customs of these vagabond sailors.

The Texas ships continued to patrol along the Mexican coast, sailing westward along the curve of the mainland and checking out the ports at Sisal, Campeche, and Laguna. On August 12, off the Tabasco bar, they overtook and captured the Mexican packet schooner *Correo de Tabasco* out of Veracruz.

The ship's dispatches turned out to be a bonanza of information, which convinced the Texans their strategy had been correct. Letters found aboard the *Correo* stated the Mexican blockading squadron was now in Veracruz, some

700 miles away from the Texas coast. There, the *General Teran*, *General Bravo*, and the former *Independence*, now recommissioned into the Mexican navy as the *Independencia*, were planning to sail in search of the hell-raising Texan flotilla. Also, on the way to reinforce them were the brigs of war *Iturbide* and *Libertador*.

The Texans continued westward still following the curve of the coast, and within a few days they anchored off the small port of Chiltepec and flew a white flag from their mastheads. A landing party was sent ashore and was met by a troop of local militia, who oozed suspicion.

When Boylan told them he only wished to return the Mexicans seized from the *Correo de Tabasco*, the fierce looks of the soldiers turned to smiles. It was a rare scene at the beach when the Texans and the Mexicans exchanged friendly greetings.

Boylan recounted, "The Commandant behaved to us in a gentlemanly way, recognized our flag and wrote a very complimentary letter to Captain Thompson for his kindness and humanity to his prisoners. He ordered his soldiers to fill our water casks and he also sent fruit and other little delicacies."

The Mexican *jefe* was also grateful for the gallantry shown to an elderly lady, the wife of a prominent Tabasco merchant, who was on board the *Correo* when it was captured.

The Texans then set sail for Veracruz in hopes they could isolate part of the Mexican squadron and destroy them, but "adverse winds" hampered their beat to the northwest. On August 17 Boylan captured the schooner *Rafaelia* and with a prize crew aboard dispatched it to Galveston.

On August 25, off Brazos de Santiago and short of rations and water, the crew was facing exhaustion from the many exertions of their successful sweep of the Mexican

Chapter 6

coast from the Yucatan to the mouth of the Rio Grande. Thompson, observing the dulling eyes of his men and an unusual lethargy in their movements, decided to return home. Their cruise had stretched more than 1,200 miles across the steaming hot Gulf Coast from Galveston to Cozumel, dodging treacherous shoals, fighting sudden vicious storms, shelling ports, fighting sea battles, and denuding the coast of Mexican shipping. Most important, they had also drawn most of the blockading fleet away from the Texas coast.

Tragically, on August 26, the returning Texans encountered a summer storm while approaching Galveston, and the *Rafaelia* was lost at sea with all hands. The following day the storm subsided, and on the morning of August 27, the *Brutus* dropped anchor in Galveston Bay. Boylan furled sails, squared yards, and granted most of his crew a long cherished shore leave. The *Invincible* anchored outside the bar.

At noon the masthead lookout on the *Invincible* reported three ships racing toward the port entrance. When they came closer, the ships were identified as the Texas brigantine *Sam Houston* fleeing from two Mexican gun brigs. The merchant vessel made it safely into Galveston harbor, but the action was just beginning.

Thompson later reported, "I immediately got under way and beat up for them with all my guns and men prepared for close action—the cannon well charged with round, grape, canister and chain shot."

Like most Texas skippers, whether from arrogance, self-confidence, or reckless bravery, Thompson did not concern himself with odds. For the two enemy ships were gun brigs, bigger, with larger crews and an overwhelming advantage in firepower.

Notwithstanding the Mexican's advantages, Thompson attacked. "I made all sail and closed with them as much as possible. I got within grape and canister distance and gave them one broadside from the larboard battery—this seemed to frighten them away—the leeward brig being a little astern, my only method was to up helm and wear round—this relieved my starboard guns then under water."

When his guns came to bear, Thompson fired another broadside, and "The shot they received immediately put them to flight."

Thompson continued, "They hauled their wind that they might get close to one another. Then they opened their fire on me, though to little effect, their shot flew over and under us in every direction, but not a man was hurt or a spar of ours cut away. Our Long Tom spoke the Texan language and almost every shot told well, and with a small assistance rendered to me the two brigs of war would have been ours."

The lookout in the *Brutus* had also spotted the enemy brigs and reported it to Captain Boylan. There then followed a tragic comedy of errors. With most of his crew still on shore leave, Boylan sent his ship's boats "to all the vessels in the harbor and obtained a number of volunteers." With a scratch crew he ordered all sails set and raced out of the harbor to give Thompson his "small assistance."

But an ebbing tide and an outgoing tidal current lowered the water level over the bar and, as Boylan recounted, "Unfortunately our vessel ran aground."

Boylan signaled for help to a nearby steamboat, the *Branch T. Archer*, and the boat "came alongside and endeavored to extricate us from our disagreeable situation." Dr. Branch T. Archer, after whom the plucky little steamer was named, had come to Texas in 1831 after killing a man in a duel, took part in the revolution, and later became secretary of war during the administration of Mirabeau B. Lamar.

Chapter 6

Captain Ross of the steamer ordered a seaman to toss a line to the stranded sailing ship, but as Boylan lamented, "The hawser unfortunately passed across our stern slightly touching the rudder."

As the heavy rope curled around the rudder, that vital part of the ship proved rotten and ripped loose from the hull. Now the *Brutus* was not only stranded, but even if she got loose from the bar, she couldn't be steered.

Still trying to get into the fight, Boylan and his volunteers transferred to the steamer. Although the *Branch T. Archer* carried no big guns, many of the volunteers were armed with their squirrel rifles. So eager for the fray, the little steamer, paddlewheels churning, dashed out to the battle.

Thompson, meanwhile, feigned a retreat from the two brigs and "hauled for the bar with the hope of enticing them into shoal water where I could have managed them better. They smelt a rat and as cowards sneaked off."

It was probably not cowardice. It is unknown if the two Mexican brigs were skippered by Britishers, who while excellent seamen, like many mercenaries proved loath to become decapitated by a Texan cannon ball. Also, their gun crews were usually untrained in naval gunnery, and most of their broadsides resulted in only making large water splashes. Aside from that, the Mexican version of the battle was quite different from Thompson's.

Thompson's attempt to lure the Mexicans inshore, however, caused his undoing. His swift maneuvering of the *Invincible* caused her rudder, also rotted out, to break loose.

Unable to be steered, the schooner floundered in waters ruffled by an onshore wind and an outgoing current. Before Thompson could get an anchor to hold, a counter current drove her inside the bar and slammed her up against a sandy bank where pounding waves began to smash against her rotting timbers.

Captain Ross and his steamer tried to save her, but Thompson said, "All proved ineffectual as she could not stand any kind of thumping and she soon went under." The steamer successfully took the crew to safety. Then she returned to the still stranded *Brutus*. After "considerable exertion" she pulled her off the bar, and when she was once more afloat, towed her to the navy yard where she was safely moored. Several weeks later a severe gale ripped across the bay, destroying more than a dozen vessels while most of the city of Galveston was flooded. Sadly, during the storm, the gallant *Brutus* was pounded to pieces and sunk.

During the battle outside the harbor, the Mexicans later claimed that Thompson was actually trying to escape from them and that the *Invincible* lost her rudder crossing the bar.

Whatever the truth, with the *Independence* captured, the *Invincible* sunk, the *Liberty* sold for debt, and the *Brutus* destroyed, the Texas navy ceased to exist.

But it got worse. If the leaders of the bold and successful cruise of the two Texas schooners expected to be greeted as conquering heroes by their president, they were rudely surprised.

A furious and unforgiving Sam Houston, in early October 1837, had Secretary Fisher impeached and removed from office. The move created an uproar in the Senate. William Wharton, the former Texas representative to the United States, with the indignities of his Mexican imprisonment still fresh on his mind, raged. Referring to Houston he said:

"That bloated mass of inebriety and insanity, of hypocrisy, vanity and villainy, when I see him sitting like an incubus and weighing down the hopes and paralyzing the energies of our infant republic... my soul sickens and I turn with horror from the scene."

On October 11 the Senate disapproved Fisher's removal, stating that the action was "disrespectful, dictatorial and indicative of a disposition on the part of the Executive [Houston] to annihilate those co-ordinate powers conferred on the Senate by the constitution." On October 18 they ordered Houston to reinstate Fisher.

Houston replied with a summary of charges against Fisher stating:

He was "trading tobacco for horses and mules with the enemy from or protected by navy vessels, using money for sales of navy vessels for personal loans, 'taking a cruise with the navy' and commanding naval vessels without orders in which the property of innocent Mexican citizens was destroyed, disobeyed orders and used the threat of the navy for release of Texan prisoners in Matamoros and criticizing the President." There was what might be called a Clintonesque legalism to most of his charges.

The Texas Senate found Fisher innocent of all charges but agreed that to keep harmony in the state government, he should resign. Conforming to the Senate's wishes, Fisher sent in his resignation.

The issue of Fisher's reinstatement as secretary of the navy arose again in 1838 when Mirabeau B. Lamar became the new president of Texas. Fisher, however, was shot dead in Matagorda after quarreling with another man.

Hot-tempered Commodore Thompson was faced with a court-martial for embezzlement, for selling the *Union*, and for the capture of the *Eliza Russell*, which with great apologies had been returned to its British owners. Among the myriad of charges Houston had leveled against him was the accusation that after the capture of the brig *Correo de*

Mexico, he had taken "for his own use six pair of pantaloons and fourteen shirts."

Exhausted after his fighting cruise, Thompson, the scourge of the enemy coast, foiled Houston's wrath by dying of a fever on November 1, 1837, before he could be brought to trial.

On October 4 Captain Boylan was ordered arrested, but Houston relented and failed to press charges against him. He probably feared such action against the intrepid skipper of the *Brutus* would cause political unrest among the many Texans who considered him a hero. Fired as an officer in the Texas navy, Boylan would re-emerge three years later as a key ally of another Texas commodore.

If storms, dangerous shoals, and Mexican men-of-war had destroyed the ships of the first Texas navy, Sam Houston on two occasions had destroyed the careers of the republic's best naval commanders. It would not be the last time.

Chapter 7

The New Navy and Old Troubles

During the final days of 1837, the 370 miles of Texas coastline lay naked of seaborne defenses. The Texas Congress, in a state of panic, ignored Sam Houston's self-induced hatred of the navy and on November 4, 1837, passed a sweeping statute creating a new navy, twice as large as the first one.

The new fleet would be formidable enough to prevent any seaborne invasion of Texas by the Mexican army and would have enough gun power to break any Mexican blockade of the republic's ports.

The problem, however, was that it would take almost two years to build and fit out the ships. During that hiatus it was known that Mexican strategists believed Texas could be reconquered, not by trudging through the wastes of South Texas, but by a full-scale invasion transported by the Mexican navy.

If the winds were favorable, their ships could bring troops, guns, ammunition, horses, food, and water the 270 miles from Matamoros to Galveston in two days. For even the most heavily laden and slow sailing troop or supply ship could make five knots with the favorable northerly set to Gulf currents.

Traveling the same distance by land, across arid ground, bad roads, lacking in forage and water, and harassed by Texas cavalry, it could take an invading army two to four weeks, if the rivers were low.

Since there were no bridges over rivers and fords were few, Texas cavalry could be depended upon to burn any ferryboats in the army's path. If there was timber available, rafts and ferries could be constructed, but much tedious loading and unloading would be required as those devices could not support loaded wagons or pack trains.

Santa Anna had made this trek in March 1836. It took him seventeen days to move a small army 300 miles from his Mexican base at Monclova to San Antonio and the Alamo. Although he made an unusually rapid forced march, averaging almost 18 miles each day, his troops arrived exhausted, many of his horses died, and he left behind his heavy artillery. Luckily for him, the rivers were not yet flooded from spring rains.

After his victory at the Alamo, on March 29 his army trekked another 200 miles to Harrisburg. They arrived there on April 20 after an exhausting march of 22 days. It was perhaps exhaustion as much as carelessness that caused the Mexican army to be annihilated at San Jacinto on April 21. Mexican generals swore they would not make the same mistakes twice.

Santa Anna, Mexican military authorities agreed, had been a damned fool. The death knell of Texas independence would be rung by first strangling their commerce by blockade and then launching a seaborne invasion. There was, they knew, nothing the Texans could do to stop them.

Chapter 7

But to paraphrase a maxim of Napoleon Bonaparte, "It is better to be lucky than smart." Texas got lucky. Three outside forces saved the young republic.

During 1838 the United States government was not prepared to allow Mexican naval ships to seize American merchant ships trading with Texas. To that end, United States naval vessels patrolled the Texas coast, putting an end to the Mexican blockade.

Secondly, during that year, the states of Yucatan, Tabasco, and Chiapas rose in revolt against the government in Mexico City and declared their independence. This alone was enough to keep the Mexican navy more than busy.

The final blow, which was to ultimately paralyze Mexican sea power and strangle their commerce, was first struck ten years previously in 1828. In that year a starving band of Mexican soldiers attacked a French pastry shop in the little town of Parian.

Breaking into the heavenly smelling bakery, they pushed the proprietor aside and gobbled up chocolate eclairs, sweet breads, and all the other delicacies of the French confectioner. The baker, shocked by this barbarian act, appealed to the French government for redress.

There were other incidents. In an affray at Atenzingo in 1833, five Frenchmen were beheaded, quartered, and their bloody parts tied to the tails of horses and driven through town to the cry of "*Mueran los estrangeros.*" And in 1835 two Frenchmen were shot after a filibuster attack on Tampico was defeated by local militia.

But to France's stupid king Louis Philippe, the crisis came when Mexico halted payments on foreign loans. For the chocolate eclairs and other debts, the French demanded a payment of 600,000 pesos.

The Mexicans refused to pay. The French king then dispatched twenty-six ships of war and 4,000 soldiers to

Mexican waters. Their fleet quickly cleared the Mexican coast of ships and blockaded Veracruz. Most importantly, they captured most of the Mexican navy, including a corvette, three brigs, and two schooners.

Outraged, the Mexicans labeled this farce the "*Guerra de los Pasteles*" or "The Pastry War."

On November 27, 1838, the one-armed French Admiral Charles Baudin ordered an attack on the Mexican fortress of San Juan de Ulloa. The fort, considered impregnable by the Mexicans, was built on an island in Veracruz harbor and was defended by 160 big guns and more than 5,000 troops.

At 2 o'clock in the afternoon the massed French fleet opened fire; by dusk they had smashed the fortifications into rubble and killed or wounded 600 defenders. A white flag went up from the ruins, and the Mexican garrison surrendered. Following the disaster, the Mexican government agree to pay the 600,000 pesos.

If people were not being maimed and killed, what happened next might have been written as a satire for Paris' Opera Comique.

The French turned down the 600,000-peso offer, hiked their demands to 800,000 pesos, and landed 3,000 troops in an attempt to capture Veracruz.

Out of forced retirement, Santa Anna rushed to Veracruz and upon his own authority assumed command of the Mexican forces. Unfortunately, as at San Jacinto, he was in repose when a French surprise attack burst into the Mexican barracks. Whether he was in *flagante delicto* with another lady is not recorded, but it was reported he escaped by running out of the barracks and down an alley clad only in his underpants.

But never lacking in courage, he found a pair of pants and a sword and rallied the retreating Mexican troops. Although indelicately clad for a Mexican general, he led a charge that drove the French invaders back to their boats and thence to the safety of their warships. During the fighting he was wounded in the left leg, and in compensation, he was heralded as "The Hero of Veracruz."

After this rebuff, the French, back on their ships, announced they had reconsidered and would accept the 600,000 pesos after all. The Mexicans agreed, the money was paid, the French fleet left the Gulf of Mexico, and Santa Anna's leg became infected and was amputated.

Again a hero, Santa Anna again became the head of the Mexican government. The leg was given a formal military funeral, and amidst the blaring of bugles, the beating of drums, and lines of saluting soldiers, it was finally buried.

For the Texans, the war of the French pastry had given them almost a year of reprieve.

On December 10, 1838, Mirabeau Buonaparte Lamar, who had commanded the Texas cavalry at San Jacinto, was inaugurated as the second president of the Texas republic. And unlike land-locked Houston, Lamar realized the strategic necessity for a strong navy and gave it his full support.

During the spring of 1839, the new Texas ships began to arrive. The steam packet *Charleston*, idled in Baltimore harbor, was purchased and rechristened *Zavala* in honor of Lorenzo de Zavala, the recently deceased former vice president of Texas. The steamship was a welcome addition because, as Commodore Moore wrote:

"She adds greatly to the efficiency of our force, particularly on the coast of Mexico, where there is for so great a portion of the time very little wind, unless it is blowing a gale."

The first and only steamship of the Texas navy, the *Zavala* displaced 569 tons and was capable of a speed of 16 knots. She was fitted out with eight guns including four 12-pounders and a long range 9-pounder. With a crew of 17

The New Navy and Old Troubles

Mirabeau Buonaparte Lamar, the second president of the Texas Republic, realized the strategic necessity for a strong navy to dominate the Gulf of Mexico. He gave the new Texas navy his full support. (Texas State Library and Archives Commission)

officers and 123 sailors and marines, she arrived in Galveston in March.

Six additional ships were purchased in Baltimore. The *Austin*, designated the flagship of the new fleet, was a large, 600-ton sloop with a big punch. She carried sixteen 24-pounders and four 18-pounders and was sailed by a crew of 23 officers and 151 sailors and marines.

Two 400-ton brigs, the *Wharton* and the *Archer*, each equipped with fifteen 18-pounders and crews of 15 officers and 123 sailors and marines, soon joined the fleet.

Chapter 7

The 600-ton Texas sloop-of-war *Austin* was the flagship of the Texas navy. It was armed with sixteen 24-pounder and four 18-pounder cannon. The *Austin* bore the brunt of the fighting during the battles off Campeche. (Harry Ransom Humanities Research Center. The University of Texas at Austin)

Three shoal-draft schooners, the *San Jacinto, San Antonio,* and *San Bernard*, of 170 tons each mounting four 12-pounders with crews of 13 officers and 69 sailors, completed the fighting ships of the second Texas navy. A 95-ton schooner used as a tender, the *Louisville* was purchased in September 1839.

President Lamar now had the ships, but he wondered, where were the sailors and most of all, where were the officers to command the fleet? The captains of the first Texas navy were either dead or disgraced.

Texas got lucky again when Lamar selected twenty-nine-year-old Edwin Ward Moore as his commodore to command the new fleet.

Moore had entered the United States Navy as a fifteen-year-old midshipman and had risen over the years to the rank of senior lieutenant. He was stocky, five-foot-eight in

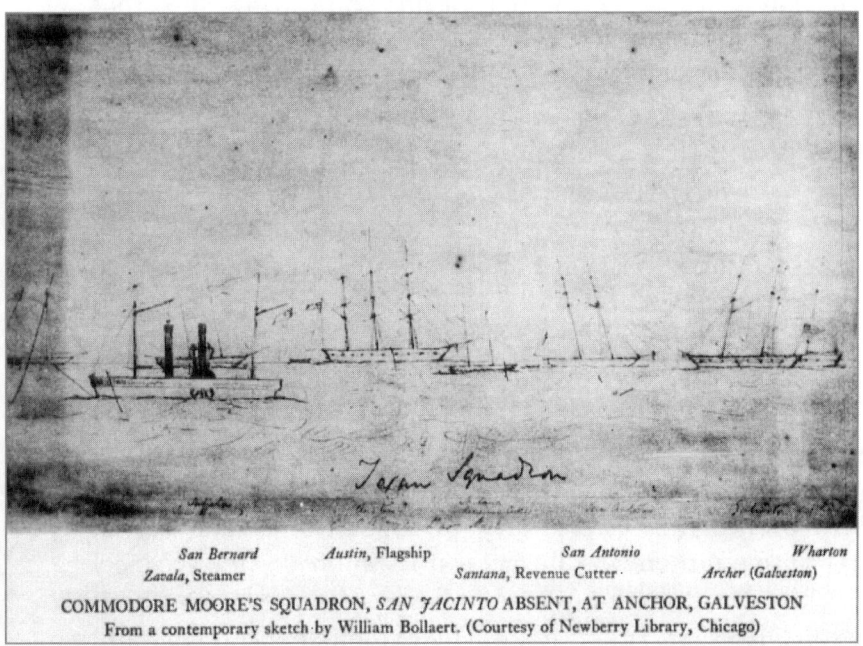

COMMODORE MOORE'S SQUADRON, *SAN JACINTO* ABSENT, AT ANCHOR, GALVESTON
From a contemporary sketch by William Bollaert. (Courtesy of Newberry Library, Chicago)

Commodore Moore's Texas navy squadron at anchor at Galveston was sketched by William Bollaert, an Englishman who enlisted in a Galveston militia unit during a Mexican invasion. (Courtesy of Newberry Library, Chicago)

height, with clear blue eyes and light brown hair. He was an excellent and meticulous sailor, who insisted that vessels be kept "ship-shape and in Bristol fashion." He was also amiable in disposition and proved to be a leader who fostered loyalty in his men.

Realizing that the United States Navy was still commanded by the aging captains of the War of 1812, he thirsted for promotion and a chance for distinction.

Chapter 7

He was serving as an officer aboard the USS *Boston* when in May 1838 they sailed into Galveston harbor. He must have envisioned future opportunity, even in the ramshackle condition of the harbor and the rotting ships that were half sunk and strewn around the harbor. In March 1839 he went on leave and returned to Galveston.

At this time he was offered command of the Texas navy. President Lamar assured him that both he and the legislature were advocates of a strong navy and that Sam Houston was finally out of office. With those assurances, Moore accepted a commission as post captain and commander of the new fleet.

In July Moore resigned his commission in the United States Navy. He narrowly escaped court-martial, before his resignation was accepted, on charges that he illegally recruited American naval personnel for his new command.

Because seamen in New Orleans were aware of the failure of the first Texas navy to regularly pay its crews, recruitment there was unsuccessful. Moore traveled to New York and, although it was a violation of United States neutrality laws, recruited a sufficient number of officers and seamen to man his ships.

The monthly pay grades were appropriate for the time: lieutenants and qualified surgeons $100; boatswains $40; midshipmen $25; and petty officers $19. Marine lieutenants drew $30; sergeants $15; and corporals $9. Ordinary seamen and marine privates were expected to risk life and limb for $12 and $7 respectively. Moore as commodore received the princely sum of $200 a month.

Fortunately, Moore was able to recruit a few experienced ship's gunners, mostly British navy castoffs. There should have been a caveat, because often the pay was late and sometimes crews were not paid at all.

The New Navy and Old Troubles

The new ships and crews marked the beginning of a professional naval service for the new republic. It came at an opportune time, for by 1839 armed merchantmen were no longer a successful substitute for specially designed men-of-war.

Warships required larger crew quarters than was usual for merchant vessels. This was because, in addition to sailing the ship, additional men were required to man the guns and to crew captured ships. Quarters were also required for marines needed as sharpshooters in the yards and for boarding and landing parties.

The big guns also presented difficult design problems. Most cannon were placed broadside in the hull to attain maximum effective firepower. But if the guns were placed too low, when the gun ports were opened in rough seas, they were likely to be swamped.

If set too high, their heavy weight detracted from the ship's stability. It was a fine point that required excellent ship design to create an effective fighting vessel.

There were other problems. Ship's cannon were usually made of iron, and they were often not cast at the same foundry, so the length and weight of each cannon might have considerable variance. And most important, the diameter of the gun barrel and muzzle was not always of the narrow tolerance that was needed for good accuracy in shooting.

Gunpowder quality was uneven, and while one keg of powder might cause a gun to overshoot a target, the next keg might cause a shot to fall short.

By 1840, however, technological changes in gunnery and steam-driven ships were threatening to make the new Texas navy obsolete even at its birth. In the beginning of the decade, Henri Joseph Paixhans, a French general, had

Chapter 7

developed a gun that would fire an explosive shell to great distances with improved accuracy.

Ominously, the Mexican navy was also frantically planning to expand their naval power. Texas agents in London reported that Mexican officials were openly shopping for powerful steam corvettes, frigates, and other large ships. They would, the reports stated, be armed with the new Paixhan guns whose explosive shells could shred rigging and turn a deck crew into a pile of bloody corpses. They were also hiring experienced naval officers, often British, to man their fleet.

Fortunately for the Texans there were interminable delays in the Mexican program because of financial distress and political revolts raging in different areas of that country. For a time, at least, the Gulf Coast was a strategic vacuum.

During this hiatus, the Texas fleet continued refitting in Galveston port. A newly appointed midshipman, Cornelius Cox, later wrote of the port, "The population probably didn't exceed 2,000, the houses were plain wooden structures... wharves had not been built, passengers (departing from ships) disembarked from boat to shore."

Recounting that ships wrecked from storms littered the port, he wrote, "One schooner was imbedded in the sand... another over on the Gulf side of the island.... But our new navy rode at anchor in the harbor and made cheerful the otherwise gloomy prospect."

Those who manned the fleet were a mixed bag. According to Cox, "Our Lieutenant commanding was the most tyrannical officer... and some of our men were real land lubbers."

Training was harsh. "To run up the rigging and out on the yard arms, and swing yourself like a monkey by one hand and balance yourself on a rope forty feet in the air and furl and unfurl sails like an old tar was just what the recruit could not do.

"And for every blunder, poor Jack would have to come down and lay himself across the gun and receive a dozen [lashes] from the boatswain's mate."

The fourteen-year-old midshipman was, however, impressed by "Commodore Moore who was the best swimmer that I ever saw. He could float like a feather in the water and swim on his back as fast as most men can the ordinary way.

"I have seen him leap from the top of the wheel house of the *Zavala*, some twenty feet above the water, and go to the bottom, a run of about forty feet."

But while the ships were fitting out and crews were paid their wages on time for a change, the Texas Legislature made an about face.

In the elections of November 1839, the Texas navy's most formidable opponent, Sam Houston, won a seat in the Fourth Legislature. Still having a large personal following, Houston began a campaign against all of President Lamar's policies, including the new navy.

He and his supporters haggled over the appointment of officers and over the cost of maintaining the fleet. In February 1840 a Naval Bill was passed that more than decimated Commodore Moore's command.

The bill provided that the two big-gunned ships, the steam-driven *Zavala* and the flagship *Austin*, the most powerful ship in the fleet, and the two large brigs *Wharton* and *Archer* were to be put "in ordinary." This meant they would by unmanned and laid up in idleness in the harbor.

Only the smaller schooners *San Jacinto*, *San Antonio*, and *San Bernard* were to be placed on active duty, and their only responsibilities would be to police the coast and prevent smuggling. If, however, Mexico should launch a fresh

Chapter 7

attack on Texas, the president was given authority to send the entire fleet to sea.

It is doubtful if the legislature ever passed a bill containing more blinding stupidity than this.

Every strategic lesson that had been so decisively demonstrated since 1835 had apparently been forgotten or perhaps never registered in the minds of the Sam Houston adherents.

The possible motives for Houston's antipathy for the navy could have resulted from a variety of reasons.

A man of great personal vanity, he had been outraged by what he considered insubordination and treason by former Secretary of the Navy Fisher, and he continued to hold a stubborn grudge against the navy.

Perhaps he believed that an active navy would inhibit peace negotiations with Mexico. But to believe that through diplomatic effort the Mexican government would give up its attempt to regain sovereignty over Texas was sheer folly.

Others believed that Houston's limited military experience had clouded his judgment. He fought in the battle of Horseshoe Bend against the Creek Indians, never rising above the rank of lieutenant. And at the decisive moment at San Jacinto, he was finally forced by his officers to give battle.

In both campaigns, volunteers, usually unpaid, constituted the main fighting forces. Houston had never faced the reality of the expenses required to maintain a regular army or navy. And like many others of his time, he believed that a country could successfully fight professional troops with volunteer militia, the experiences of the War of the Revolution and the War of 1812 notwithstanding.

Another school of thought believed that Houston hoped Texas would be quickly annexed by the United States and could depend for safety on her naval power. A Texas fleet

The New Navy and Old Troubles

The Texas navy recruited experienced sailors when possible but often had to settle for inexperienced but tough frontiersmen to fill its ranks. (Texas State Library and Archives Commission)

would then be unnecessary. But in 1839 the possibility of annexation seemed dim. Anti-slavery forces in the American government, led by former president John Quincy Adams, vigorously opposed annexation, considering it a plot designed to increase the number of slave states in the Union.

Neither president Andrew Jackson nor Martin Van Buren believed they were strong enough politically to force an annexation bill through Congress. Texas would be on its own for another decade.

A more simplistic view of Houston's lack of maritime vision was that, like many Americans from insular states, he simply didn't understand the economic, political, and military value of a fleet in being. Sadly, his lack of understanding of the contribution of the Texas navy to the independence of the Texas republic has been shared by most

Chapter 7

modern historians. To President Lamar's credit, he ignored the Naval Bill and kept the ships intact and ready for sea.

While discouraged by the Naval Bill, Commodore Moore, a hands-on and industrious commander, continued to roam throughout his fleet, fixing, adjusting, and teaching some of his more inexperienced officers.

One glaring problem with the equipment given his schooners was discovered during shake-down cruises in the Gulf. It soon became apparent that the anchors furnished to the ships were too light to hold during the sudden squalls that came roaring down from the north during the winter months and from the south during the summer. Not only were the anchors too light, but the anchor lines lacked the strength to withstand the great strains put on them in stormy weather.

Sadly, there were no funds to buy heavier anchors and lines. It was a problem unsolved and one that would in the future haunt the three schooners.

Routine escorting of merchant vessels by the schooners and yeoman work by the *Zavala* in towing sailing ships across the shifting channels of the Galveston bar proved excellent training for the new ships. But the fleet's sailors were growing restive.

Many of the new crews had signed on with the lure of prize money to be divvied up from the capture of Mexican vessels. Others had volunteered for reasons of patriotism or a desire for a fighting adventure. Not surprisingly, disciplinary problems were on the increase.

In an attempt to prevent desertions, Moore kept his ships anchored out in the bay and shore leave was rarely granted. On May 9 a marine was shot to death while trying to desert. On the following night three sailors crept up onto the deck of the *San Jacinto*, lowered the captain's gig into the water, climbed in, and rowed to shore. A boatswain's mate was arrested and thrown into the brig for insolence to a superior officer. And there was a rumor that officers on the *Austin* were planning to steal the ship, hoist the Jolly Roger, and sail off on a pirating expedition.

The rumor turned out to be false, but it was an indication of the frustration felt by a band of men who wanted to fight but were chained to routine duties.

President Lamar, meanwhile, seized a loophole in the onerous Naval Bill. He received news that Mexico had purchased a steam-driven man-o-war in Great Britain. There was also evidence that General Mariano Arista had assisted Comanche Indian attacks on settlers on the Texas frontier. Based on those reports, Lamar believed he was justified in sending the full fleet to sea. Further justification came when the president of Mexico in April 1840 proclaimed a blockade of Texas ports.

Fortunately for Texas, during the summer of 1840 a new revolt was breaking out in the Yucatan. The merchants and ship owners in those ports were furious with the government in Mexico City, whose policies they deemed both stupid and stubborn. Their follies had brought down the French navy onto their coast, leading to the capture of their ships, the wiping out of their seaborne commerce, and the bankruptcy of their economy. Aside from the French incursions, the Yucatan merchants were still smarting from the raids of Texas privateers like the *Thomas Toby*. If Mexico could not protect them, they determined they would protect themselves. One form of insurance, they believed, was to make an alliance with the pugnacious new Republic of Texas. In this revolt, President Lamar sensed an opportunity.

Chapter 8

Scurvy, Storms, and a Silver Ransom

During the summer of 1840, President Lamar drafted a draconian letter of instructions to James Treat, the diplomatic agent of the Texas Republic, in Mexico City. Treat was, at that time, engaged in fruitless negotiations to secure Mexican recognition of Texas independence.

Lamar instructed Treat to deliver an ultimatum to the Mexican government stating that if within ten days they did not recognize Texas independence, he would break off all negotiations. The letter was, in effect, an invitation to go to war.

Lamar ordered Commodore Moore to send one of his warships to Veracruz to deliver the letter to Treat. The rest of the fleet, Lamar ordered, was to put to sea. If Mexico ignored the ultimatum or broke the de facto truce prevailing at the moment, the commodore was to negotiate a treaty with the Yucatan rebels. With his Yucatan allies, he was then to take aggressive action against Mexican ports and shipping.

Scurvy, Storms, and a Silver Ransom

On July 22, 1840, the flagship *Austin*, steamship *Zavala*, and the schooners *San Jacinto* and *San Bernard* put to sea, headed for Mexican waters. Freshly outfitted, the crews wore jaunty straw hats with a wide brim, white cotton shirts, a red scarf around their necks, and vests of white duck.

In their ditty bags they had a waterproof hat made of oilskin or canvas with a broad brim behind to protect the neck during bad weather. For cold weather, they were issued warm pea jackets and red flannel shirts.

Boarding parties were armed with a slightly curved, basket hilted cutlass, 30 inches in length, and a brace of the new 5-shot Colt revolvers, later made famous by the Texas Rangers.

From their mastheads they flew the new Texas national flag. It was of similar design to the flag of the United States of America. It featured a blue perpendicular stripe of the width of one-third of the whole length of the flag. Centered in the blue field was a large five-pointed white star. Two horizontal stripes of equal breadth, the upper stripe white, the lower red, stretched across the length of the flag. It was the famous Lone Star Flag of the Lone Star Republic.

With an opportunity for action and at last the full support of their government, the officers and men were jubilant. Enthusiastic and light-hearted, sailing swiftly over sunlit waters, they might well have echoed the words of the crew of Gilbert and Sullivan's HMS *Pinafore*:

> We sail the ocean blue
> And our saucy ships are beauties
> We're sober men and true
> And attentive to our duty

and paraphrasing, Moore might have added:

Chapter 8

> I am the Captain of the *Austin*
> And a right good Captain too
> .... And be it understood
> I command a right good crew.

The voyage was uneventful except when Lieutenant Armstrong J. Lewis of the *San Bernard*, while looking upward to give an order to sailors aloft in the rigging, stepped off the cabin trunk and fell down a hatchway, breaking his leg.

A few days later C.S. Nash, an ordinary seaman, died of dropsy, and an older seaman died of unknown causes. In October seaman S.O. Sawyer fell from the foretop gallant yard overboard and was lost. At times the Texas navy was a cruel mistress.

A sailor's life was dangerous, the food poor, punishment harsh, and medical attention usually nonexistent. There was always the danger of scurvy, arthritis, pneumonia, tuberculosis, dysentery, vermin bites, and perennially, yellow fever and malaria. And if you were not swept overboard and drowned, you could be disemboweled by a cannon ball. As Doctor Johnson once remarked, "No man will be a sailor who has contrivance enough to get himself into a jail."

Young Midshipman C.C. Cox wrote:

"The life is a hard one, the discipline rigid, a boy of the age of 14 or 15 has not physical capacity to perform the regular watch on seaboard, four hours on duty and eight off.... In case of dereliction of duty for officers the usual punishment is four hours on and four off.

"But when one of the seamen committed an offense or violated an order, the punishment was frightful. Flogging was a common pastime, a daily occurrence.... Grave offences were rewarded with the 'Cat of 9 tails,' three dozen licks on the bare back was the usual dose.

"The culprit stood at the gangway, with his hands lashed to the rigging, his feet fastened to a grating on which he stood. The man was stripped to the waist—all hands were on deck to witness the scene—the articles of war read, the ship's physician on one side and the boatswain on the other.

"At each stroke of the lash the solemn count was proclaimed aloud and the poor criminal would skringe [sic] and grunt at every blow. By the time three dozen were given, the fellow's back was variegated with the colors red, black, blue and white, and the blood running in little rivers at his feet."

Lamar's dispatches to Treat were put aboard the *San Jacinto*, which, making a fast passage, arrived off Veracruz by August 1. The dispatches were sent ashore and entrusted to British legation officials, who delivered them to Treat in mid-August. Following their delivery, the *San Jacinto* was instructed to hover off Veracruz for at least thirteen days awaiting a response from the Texas agent.

In the meantime, Moore and the other ships had arrived at the Yucatan port of Sisal on July 31. Moore found the Yucatan navy to consist of only "one small brig and two schooners," under the command of the redoubtable Captain James D. Boylan, the former skipper of the Texas warship *Brutus*. It became obvious to Moore that if the Yucatan rebellion was to be successful, their leaders must forge an alliance with the Texas fleet.

While the Texans and the Yucatan leaders planned strategy, the young men of the fleet occupied themselves with more romantic notions. Cox said:

"Many ladies came to visit the ship. I thought the Mexican girls beautiful. They all smoked and each carried a little bunch of cigaritas. The etiquette was to place a cigarita in the mouth, light it and then hand it to the other party. This temptation very few young men can resist."

Chapter 8

On a more serious level, Moore ordered the *Zavala* to establish a base for the fleet in the Arcas Islands, one hundred miles to the west of Sisal.

The Arcas consisted of three coral islands, positioned in a triangle, named Triangulo Oeste, Triangulo Este, and Triangulo Sud. They were located approximately 120 miles northwest of Campeche and rose to an elevation of only twenty-one feet above sea level. They were uninhabited except for gannets, sea gulls, and other assorted coastal birds that laid their eggs on the sandy beaches.

The islands provided a relatively safe anchorage, except in the event of a hurricane, and offered a secluded rendezvous for the fleet as well as an opportunity for shore parties to feel dry land under their feet, without presenting any possibility of desertion.

Cox described the islands, saying:

"There was a small but beautiful body of water in the center which affords a safe harbor for vessels drawing 20 to 30 feet. We anchored in about three fathoms, 200 yards from shore.

"The water is very clear, objects on the bottom being clearly seen. We had fine fishing...we collected beautiful specimens of coral...it was delightful bathing in this saltwater lake. There is almost no vegetation on the islands... but we captured a great many eggs and young birds to eat."

Most importantly, sea breezes swept the island, keeping the climate dry and free of the swarms of mosquitoes that spread malaria and the dreaded yellow fever on the mainland from Matamoros to the Yucatan.

Meanwhile, Moore continued negotiations with Santiago Mendez, the rebel governor of Yucatan, who offered the use of his state's ports to the Texas navy.

The Arcas and the Yucatan ports were vital if the Texans were to maintain constant pressure on the Mexican Gulf coast. From Galveston to the major Mexican port of Veracruz, it was more than 600 miles. And from New Orleans, the nearest friendly port where a ship could undergo major repairs, it was almost 800 miles.

But from Campeche, where fresh water and provisions could be obtained and minor repairs and supplies could be secured, it was only 300 miles from the Mexican naval base at Veracruz. And from the Arcas, Veracruz was only 270 miles away.

Operating from these bases and blessed with favorable winds, the Texas fleet would be able, within a two-day sail, to cut off all seaborne supplies to Mexico City.

Unless the Mexican government could acquire a fleet that could defeat the Texas flotilla, they were in danger of having their commerce strangled.

On August 23 Moore, who was aboard the *Austin*, joined the *San Jacinto*, which was cruising three miles off Veracruz in hopes of receiving a message from Treat. The following day the British navy brig *Penguin* sailed out of the harbor and hailed the Texas ships. The British captain handed over letters from Treat to President Lamar and members of his cabinet.

He informed Moore that Treat had failed to deliver the ultimatum and still hoped for a diplomatic solution. He also confirmed that the Mexican government had purchased a sloop-of-war, the *Iguala*, from the French, and was planning on buying another warship. They had also acquired the steamship *Argyle* now in Veracruz harbor. The Mexican government was, he said, rapidly acquiring a new and formidable navy.

On August 25 Moore sent the *San Jacinto* to Galveston to deliver Treat's dispatches. Frustrated and champing at the bit for offensive action, Moore wrote a series of letters to Lamar complaining that Treat had assured the Mexican

Chapter 8

government the Texans would not attack while negotiations were still pending. In the meantime, he stated, new Mexican warships arriving from Europe would be sailing into Veracruz with their crews "laughing at us."

He declared that, at present, "Every Mexican vessel can be captured that dare put to sea, and their whole sea coast be kept in a perfect state of fear and trembling.... Now's the time to push them for they never were so prostrate."

But Treat continued to dither in fruitless negotiations and a decisive moment was lost.

Meanwhile, the *San Bernard* covered the entrance to Veracruz while the *Zavala*, having exhausted most of its coal, remained anchored off the Arcas awaiting a fresh supply of fuel.

After receiving reports that General Arista was gathering troops near Matamoros, threatening another invasion of Texas, Moore sailed the *Austin* to the mouth of the Rio Grande. Hovering off the shore with his guns run out, he caused Arista to fear a Texas seaborne invasion. To avoid a fight, which Arista believed would leave him outnumbered and outgunned, the Mexican general withdrew his troops into the interior.

By mid-September the *Austin* was sailing off Tampico when scurvy broke out among the crew. It was not surprising. The staple diet on Texas navy ships was hardly a gourmet's delight. Cox complained:

"Salt beef, salt pork, beans, tea and hard tack were the staples. Our crackers were nearly always old, musty and full of worms. The worms were easily disposed of by heating the bread and then knocking them out, or soaking the crackers in hot tea. They are easily killed and I never discovered any difference in the taste of the worms and the bread."

Scurvy, Storms, and a Silver Ransom

The sailor's diet was sorely lacking in vitamin C, and this deficiency produced the dread scurvy whose symptoms included mental depression, sallow complexion, sunken eyes, tender gums, and muscular pains. If not remedied by eating fruit, vegetables, or other foods producing ascorbic acid, degeneration set in rapidly. Teeth fell out, large-sized hemorrhages penetrated the muscles and other body parts, and diarrhea and finally kidney failure could lead to a miserable death.

Leaving the *San Antonio* to cover Tampico, Moore sailed to Lobos Island. Located sixty miles south of Tampico and covered with lime trees, Isla Lobos offered a welcome haven for the dozen scurvy-stricken sailors. Moore had his men laid out on the beach. They were covered with warm sand and fed copious amounts of lime juice and fresh turtle soup. On this rather exotic diet they began to recover rapidly. The commodore's prescriptions were perhaps unique in the history of scurvy treatment; but they worked.

On October 1 the *Austin*, which was anchored in the lee of the Lobos reefs, was struck by a sudden norther. For four days, with sails furled and oft-repeated prayers that their anchors would hold, they successfully rode out the storm. During the blow, a lookout reported that a Mexican vessel had run aground on a nearby reef. When the weather eased on October 6, Moore sent out boats that rescued the crew of the merchant brig *Segunda Fama*.

In addition to the twenty-six sailors saved, the Texans recovered a large cargo of flour. When the storm finally ended, Texas and Mexican cooks prepared a sumptuous feast of spaghetti shared by the crews of both nations.

On October 16 Moore sailed to Tampico and sent the Mexicans ashore. The people of the port were most grateful and sent boats to the *Austin* loaded with fruit, brandy, and voluminous letters of thanks. It was a kind gesture, but it

Chapter 8

gave Moore a false belief that he would be welcomed at that port. It was a mistake that later nearly caused the deaths of some of his crew.

A few days after the fruit and brandy arrived, Moore detained the outbound schooner *Conchita* and sent a longboat with a boarding party to check her manifests. On board was rebel General Pedro Lemus and his family. Lemus was under arrest for treason and was bound for Veracruz. Upon arrival, he would have faced a swift court-martial, a brisk walk to the nearest wall, and a choice of a blindfold or a cigarette before a squad of riflemen finally resolved his political problems. Moore freed the family, took them aboard, and later deposited them at a Yucatan port and safety.

Any good will gained from the rescue of the crew of the *Segunda Fama* was quickly dissipated by this act; the Mexican military was furious at Moore for freeing a man whom they considered a traitor.

Transporting the Mexican passengers had reduced the *Austin*'s fresh water supply, so on October 21 Moore sent his ship's longboat toward shore to fill their kegs. He believed that if they would not be welcomed by the military garrison, at least they would not be molested. He was wrong. As the boat approached the shore, an artillery battery opened up and started shooting at the Texans.

Midshipman James L. Mabry, observing from *Austin*, later wrote that the boat "was fired at three times and narrowly escaped destruction, the balls striking very close to her. We directed a gun at the fort and fired it, but the distance was too great."

The attack gave Moore the excuse he needed. According to his orders he could commence hostilities if attacked. He immediately ordered the *San Antonio* to patrol the waters around Veracruz and to seize every Mexican ship in the area. Happily he sent a dispatch to Treat stating he had commenced hostilities against Mexico.

Treat responded that he too had given up hope of making a peace treaty with Mexico. A few days later, while returning to Texas, he had a relapse from his chronic tuberculosis and died.

The commodore planned a systematic blockade of the entire Mexican Gulf coast. On October 20 he set sail for the Arcas Islands to collect his remaining ships. While en route, on November 2, 1840, he captured the Mexican merchant ship *Ana Maria* carrying a rich cargo of flour, coffee, and flannel.

When he arrived at the Arcas in early November, he was faced with a series of disasters. The *Zavala*, low on fuel and with the crew on half-rations, had left for parts unknown, presumably to obtain desperately needed supplies. But at least in the absence of conflicting evidence, Moore could hope for the best where the *Zavala* was concerned. Even a cursory inspection of the Arcas anchorage, however, revealed that a far more trying fate had befallen the *San Bernard* and the *San Jacinto*.

En route to the Arcas Islands, the crew of the *San Bernard* had been struck with both fever and scurvy, and only three men were fit for duty when they attempted to make an anchorage at the Arcas. Neither officers nor men were at their best, and during their entrance they went aground and tore loose some copper plates protecting their hull. Lieutenant William S. Williamson and the few fit men, with Herculean efforts, managed to get her off the reef, sail her into the center of the three islands, and drop anchor.

Two of the crew subsequently died, and the remainder, nearly comatose, lay idly at their anchorage, trying to regain their strength.

Chapter 8

To make matters even worse, on October 9 the *San Jacinto* sailed into the Arcas, hoping to make a safe anchorage in the lagoon. Upon approaching the islands, they signaled to the *San Bernard*, requesting an officer and a ship's boat to guide them past the reefs and into a safe berth.

Lieutenant Williamson responded by dispatching Midshipman Charles B. Underhill in a launch to guide them in. But for some reason, perhaps to shift his anchorage to accommodate the incoming *San Jacinto*, Williamson hauled his anchor and hoisted his sails. He was probably too sick to be efficient and clumsily tacked the *San Bernard* into the launch, smashing it in half and injuring two sailors.

Midshipman Underhill and his crew were picked up by the *San Jacinto*, but the young midshipman, probably still shaken by the collision, guided the schooner to an anchorage too close to the reefs.

At noon that same day, a norther swept over the islands, and the *San Jacinto*'s forward anchor began to break loose in the rough water. As the anchor began to slip, the schooner began to swing wildly and careen toward the coral reefs nearby.

Fighting the pummeling rain and roaring winds, the crew attempted to regain ground by hauling in on the stern anchor line, but the light anchor broke loose from its grip on the bottom. When the sailors heaved on the line, the anchor simply skipped along the bottom, failing to grip in the hard sand.

As the schooner began to drift toward the sharp reefs, the crew in desperation tied a line to their heaviest cannon and then pushed the improvised anchor overboard. It too failed to hold, and the ship continued drifting dangerously near the reef. Then, suddenly, the stern anchor finally gripped the bottom, but as the crew breathed a sigh of relief, the anchor line broke under the strain. Again they were adrift. As a last resort the *San Jacinto*'s desperate crew hoisted their storm jib, hoping to gain an angle to the wind so as to sail her out into the Gulf, but they were unable to make way against the screaming winds.

For almost twelve hours the crew fought valiantly to save their ship, but in pitch darkness, some time after midnight, they lost all control. The *San Jacinto* careened about, smashed into a reef, and tore a large hole in her starboard bow. In their remaining ship's boat, the crew fought their way across the swirling lagoon and made it safely to the *San Bernard*.

Two days later Moore arrived on the *Austin*. With his customary energy, he directed the crews in a salvage attempt. After pumping and bailing like demons for two days, they had reduced the water level enough to keep the *San Jacinto* afloat. Moore supervised temporary repairs to the hull but realized the ship could not stand up to heavy seas. The only course was to leave her anchored in the Arcas until he could acquire enough planking and other materials to make her seaworthy. Leaving behind a few crewmen with a supply of food and fresh water, he sailed to the Yucatan. There he delivered General Lemus and his family to safety and solidified his arrangements with the rebel government. The repaired *San Bernard* was sent to search the coast for the missing *Zavala*.

When he reached Campeche, Moore conferred with the rebel government leaders while Lemus, greeted as a hero, was named Yucatan's Secretary of War and Marine. Together, they worked out plans for mutual cooperation in a naval war against Mexico.

While loading on fresh water and provisions, Moore was informed of the travail of the *Zavala*. The steamship, under the command of Commander John Lothrop, Moore's most

Chapter 8

capable officer, had reached the Yucatan coast where fuel and provisions were obtained on credit.

On October 3 the *Zavala* was anchored two miles offshore of the Tabasco River. Lothrop was preparing to send a shore party to purchase wood to fuel his engines when the ship was struck by the same norther that had wrecked the *Segunda Fama*.

Midshipman Cox described the scene:

"About sundown... the sea was quite smooth, the sky clear and not a breath of wind. Very soon a heavy sea came rolling in from the Gulf. The strong current from the river which after entering the Gulf took a course along the land making the ship ride in the trough of the sea and she rolled from side to side like a great log."

Almost immediately, the storm-lashed waves ripped away the ship's rudder. Unable to steer, Lothrop had the anchors dropped and prayed they would hold. The blow continued for more than five days and nights, and Cox reported, "The waves were rolling in mountain high." The ship, bobbing on its anchor lines, repeatedly struck bottom in the shallow coastal waters. This strain caused the masts to break off and wash overboard.

The *Zavala* managed to hold her position by running her engines under full steam, but soon both wood and coal were used up. "Strip the ship," Lothrop commanded, and furniture, doors, masts and spars were thrown into the engines' fireboxes. When they were burned up, the ship's cabin, deck planking, and bulkheads were flung into the dying fires. Cox reported:

"It was unsafe to be on the deck without fastening yourself to something. Every moment it looked as if the next wave would upset the ship or knock her to pieces."

He added, "I was indifferent to the danger because I was so dreadful seasick."

Starting to drift toward shore, Lothrup ordered the ship's three biggest cannon lashed together and pushed over the side to increase his anchor power. When the ship listed to port, one of her paddlewheel compartments was flooded and one engine shut down.

Still drifting toward shore, Lothrup ordered all the ship's guns lashed to lines and pushed overboard. As the *Zavala* began to wallow in the foaming sea, he had all the cannonballs heaved into the waters. When all seemed lost, after three days of hell, suddenly the storm abated. The wind ceased to howl and a dead calm came over the waters.

The exhausted crew hauled up their anchors, cut the lines holding the submerged cannon, and under one engine managed to limp five miles into the small Tabasco port of Frontera. "Our handsome steamer," Cox lamented, "was almost a wreck." The young midshipman was also almost a wreck. He came down with scurvy and a spell of fever and was put ashore and "nursed by a good lady" of Frontera until he recovered.

In Frontera the ship's carpenter constructed a new rudder, a fresh supply of wood was loaded, the flooded paddlewheel compartment was drained, and the denuded cabin and the deck planks replaced. *Zavala* got up steam and Lothrop sailed her back to the scene of their desperate battle against the storm.

Strong-lunged divers located the cannon and the solid shot, fixed lines to them, and the crew hauled them to the surface and repositioned them aboard the ship. Sailing on a course for Campeche, the *Zavala*, by chance, met up with the *San Bernard*. Traveling in concert, the two ships sailed into Campeche harbor, joining Moore and the *Austin*.

His fleet now assembled, Moore planned joint action with the Yucatan forces. The rebels complained that their lucrative commercial ties with Tabasco had been severed

Chapter 8

when troops loyal to Mexico City began to overrun the state. In exchange for supplies, General Anaya proposed that Moore's fleet aid him in breaking the enemy grip on the area. In addition, Anaya promised he would exact a ransom of $25,000 from the state capital, San Juan Bautista. This too would be given to Moore in exchange for services rendered.

The commodore readily agreed, and on November 19, 1840, the *Zavala* towed the *Austin*, *San Bernard*, and a Yucatan brig up the "Tabasco" River (actually the Rio Grijalva). With 140 Yucatan troops crowding the decks, the little fleet chugged ninety miles to San Juan Bautista (now the modern city of Villahermosa). The capital, then a city of more than 10,000, was garrisoned by a force of 600 troops.

The passage was marred when the ships ran aground in the shallows and their masts became tangled with dangling tree branches. The sailing ships would sometimes start swinging erratically on the long ropes tethering them to the steamer, leading to further grounding on the river banks. But the *Zavala* always managed to tug them free.

During the trip, they chugged past steaming jungle swamps and tropical rain forests, where hidden in the jungle vegetation were the colossal stone heads. These were carved from huge basalt blocks by the ancient Olmecs, the people whose culture had once dominated the region. The marshes were so insect infested, particularly with mosquitoes carrying deadly yellow fever, that many populated areas were known as "Cities of Death."

The flotilla anchored off the capital on November 20 and promptly opened up their gun ports and ran out their heavy cannon. The Mexican commander took one look and, not being suicidal, surrendered the city and withdrew his troops.

General Anaya demanded $25,000 dollars from the city officials or, he threatened, the fleet would blow San Juan Bautista to hell. The city fathers promptly opened their coffers and produced the funds. When Anaya stalled on transferring the money to the Texans, Moore seized the Yucatan vessels and threatened to close the river to commerce until he was paid. At that, Anaya quickly paid up, and $25,000 in silver coins was brought to the Texas commodore.

A minor incident marred the triumph when it was learned that Edward Thornton, a foretops man on the *Austin*, was planning a mutiny and the theft of the ransom money. Moore held a court-martial whose quick verdict sentenced him to be hanged. Some of his officers, however, recommended that the sentence be commuted to 200 lashes. This was dubious clemency, but Thornton foiled justice by dying of yellow fever before the boatswain's mate could do his duty.

The Texans held San Juan Bautista for twenty-one days until they were struck by an epidemic of yellow fever. With few men fit for duty, Moore, who also contacted the fever, ordered the *Zavala* to tow the *Austin* and the *San Bernard* downriver to the Gulf. After reaching the Gulf, while cruising off the Tabasco port of Laguna, Moore learned that another fierce norther had struck the Arcas Islands and totally wrecked the already wounded *San Jacinto*.

The crewmen left ashore on the islands, however, were happily in better physical condition than the men in the rest of the squadron. Midshipman Alfred Walke wrote that they had enough whiskey to "Splice the main brace" on Christmas Day. Creating a potent eggnog by mixing seagull's eggs with whiskey, Walke said, "I drank to all my absent friends' health and retired [or passed out]... in a perfect state of happiness. Hurrah for the Arcas."

Chapter 8

Walke termed the islands a "paradise," and except for the lack of female companionship and the dwindling supply of whiskey, the sailors, living a Robinson Crusoe life, would have been reluctant to rejoin the fleet. But on January 13, 1841, the idyll ended when they were picked up by the *Austin*.

The flagship was sailing short handed, twenty-six of the *Austin*'s crew having died during the cruise, mostly from yellow fever. And burials at sea were all too common during the cruise. The corpse was dressed in his best clothes, then sewed up in a canvas shroud. The sail makers, who acted as undertakers, always put a strong stitch through the corpse's nose, which they sewed into the canvas. This was designed to prevent the body from breaking out of the shroud and returning to haunt the ship.

Two large cannonballs were sewn in at the feet. The body was then carried on deck and placed on a plank with one end laid on the side of the ship's rail. The crew was piped on deck, the captain read a passage from the Bible, caps were doffed, and the plank was lifted up and the body slid into the water feet first. It was a solemn ceremony, and it was even given to mutineers when they were brought down from the yardarm from which they had been hung.

The squadron continued to patrol the Mexican coast for several more months. Finally Moore turned homeward, and in February 1841 the proud but battered flotilla sailed into Galveston harbor.

Summing up his squadron's cruise in a report to Secretary of the Navy Louis P. Cooke, Moore wrote:

"The $25,000 with which supplies were obtained from New Orleans enabled the squadron to keep at sea for 10 months and thereby kept the Mexican navy from appearing off the coast of Texas to enforce their blockade.

"We remained in quiet possession of Tabasco [he meant San Juan Bautista] for 21 days and not a shot was fired at us as we were leaving.... One Mexican schooner was captured...sent to Galveston and sold for $7,000."

He might have added that the Texas fleet's support of the Yucatan rebellion had diverted Mexican forces from confrontations with Texas. The government at Mexico City had realized that it must first crush internal rebellions before it could turn its wrath against the Texans.

On another level, Texas historian Jim Dan Hill was of the opinion that Texas naval dominance in the Gulf of Mexico was a major factor in Great Britain's formal recognition of the Republic of Texas. While no major sea battles had been fought, in terms of naval strategy, the cruise had been a great success.

To the hard-worked crews, however, it was less than a financial bonanza. Midshipman Cox complained that when all the prize money was distributed, "Eight dollars was the share I got."

CHAPTER 9

Yucatan and a Mutiny

The Texas fleet's triumphal arrival in Galveston turned into yet another disappointment. Moore had expected to sail his flotilla from there to New Orleans where he would refit his ships with fresh paint and new sails. Perhaps, he hoped, he could purchase adequate anchors and anchor hawsers.

But when his fleet anchored in the bay, his first order from the new Secretary of the Navy, John G. Tod, was to lay up his flagship in ordinary, discharge most of his crews, and disband his flotilla.

The two brigs were to be laid up as well as the formidable *Zavala*. Only the two schooners *San Antonio* and *San Bernard* were to be kept shipshape, but they were relegated to making a survey of the Texas coastline or carrying dispatches.

The problem, as usual, was money. Keeping a fleet in being was expensive, and shortsighted legislators, with no concept of naval strategy and led by Sam Houston, choked off funds to maintain the ships.

As a result, many of the fleet's experienced seamen, so difficult to recruit, were laid off. The remaining men grew increasingly restive and disenchanted with the service. Deteriorating morale also affected the officers. Lieutenant James S. O'Shaunessy, the skipper of the *San Bernard*, while sailing on patrol off the coast of Mexico, found the British man-o-war *Comus* in Veracruz harbor. After bringing the *San Bernard* into the port, O'Shaunessy presented the documents declaring Great Britain's formal recognition of the independence of the Republic of Texas to the British captain.

After delivering that happy message, O'Shaunessy loaded thirty of the new and lethal Colt revolvers and a number of the new carbines into the ship's longboat. Rowing into the little harbor of Laguna de Terminos, he had the weapons unloaded and dispatched the boat back to the ship. On shore he was met by Mexican businessmen of dubious reputation. After O'Shaunessy told them he had deserted from the Texas service, he sold them the weapons for a sizable sum of money.

While the *San Bernard* was anchored near the *Comus*, a Mexican officer came aboard the British vessel with a message for the Texans. The Mexican officer requested that a British officer inform the Texans that if they did not immediately leave the harbor, they would be fired upon. For emphasis, he pointed to the shoreline where three large cannon were being hauled onto the beach, preparing to open fire.

When informed of the ultimatum, Lieutenant Armstrong I. Lewis, who had assumed command of the *San Bernard*, replied to the British captain that after the layoffs he had only twelve seamen to sail his ship. With a fresh norther blowing in, he was afraid he didn't have enough men to get under way against strong contrary winds.

Chapter 9

In a nineteenth-century version of lend-lease, the kindly British captain loaned the Texans a dozen seamen until the *San Bernard* got underway and cleared the harbor.

If those humiliations were not enough, Moore's cousin, Alexander Moore, who had been commissioned in the Texas navy, was forced to resign after he was involved in a financial scandal.

After the *San Bernard* returned to Galveston, she was given the mission of transporting another Texas peace commissioner, James Webb, a former Florida judge, back to Veracruz. His mission was to launch another vain effort to negotiate a peace treaty with the Mexican government.

The *San Bernard* arrived in Veracruz in mid-June, but when the Mexicans refused to talk with Webb, she set sail for the return passage to Galveston. Only a few miles out of the Mexican harbor, they picked up a fresh breeze, and the schooner, with a bone in her teeth, skimmed swiftly across the Gulf waters. Suddenly there was a terrible crashing sound as the ship's foretopmast broke in half and sails, spars, and rigging lines came tumbling down on the deck, injuring sailors and making a gigantic mess.

Cutting away the jumbled gear and ordering it heaved overboard, Lt. Lewis examined the broken mast and found the wood was rotten to the core. Jury-rigging a sail to the stump of the mast, they sailed on. Fortunately they were favored with good weather, and within a few days the *San Bernard* was able to limp into Galveston harbor.

From May to November 1841, Commodore Moore, aboard the *San Antonio*, had been charting the dangerous shoal waters along the Texas coastline.

One of the major drawbacks to Texas seaborne commerce had always been the very high insurance rates Lloyd's of London and other marine insurance companies levied on vessels heading for Galveston and Brazosport.

Yucatan and a Mutiny

Fierce summer storms blowing in from the Gulf of Mexico and winter northers had caused the barrier islands off the Texas coast to be littered with the wreckage of ships caught in stormy seas and driven aground.

Contributing to the maritime disasters was the fact that most of the charts used by mariners were incorrect, and many areas had never been charted at all. Moore was determined to remedy these deficiencies by making an accurate survey of the entire coast.

The commodore and his officers took thousands of soundings and sextant readings and made nautical calculations from Sabine Pass to Brownsville. They found that some existing charts were more than seventy-five miles in error and that depth soundings in and near harbors, vital for safe landings, were practically nonexistent.

When this monumental job was completed and new and accurate charts were drawn, the work was sent to a nautical publishing company in New York City. When published they made a lasting contribution to maritime safety by Moore and his officers as, with lowered insurance costs and fewer wrecks, commerce increased all along the Texas coast.

Sadly, while this important work was going on, the rest of the Texas navy was rotting in port. Tough-minded President Lamar, however, was planning a two-pronged attack on Mexico in which the navy would play a major role.

On June 19, 1841, he sent out a large trading caravan from the Austin area on a 625-mile trek to Santa Fe. The merchants were accompanied by a band of armed adventurers as the expedition was designed not only to increase trade but to sever Santa Fe and what is now northern New Mexico from allegiance to Mexico City.

Unfortunately for the Texans, everything went wrong. They strayed from the correct route and wandered aimlessly for days. Hostile Comanches raided their wagons and

Chapter 9

ran off part of their stock. They had insufficient food supplies for the men, and there was only sparse grazing for the transport animals. Most of all, they lacked fresh water.

In mid-September, after trekking more than 1,000 miles, they finally staggered into Mexican settlements near Santa Fe. Expecting to be greeted enthusiastically by local authorities, they were surrounded instead by a large force of Mexican cavalry, which took the entire caravan prisoner. The trading goods were confiscated, and the Texans were arrested and marched to Mexico City in chains. They were not finally released until April 1842.

But if the land prong of Lamar's strategy was a disaster, he held high hopes his navy would succeed in breaking up Mexico's attempts to conquer Texas.

On September 17, 1841, he negotiated a formal alliance with rebellious Yucatan. The agreement called for Texas to send three or more warships to Yucatan to fend off Mexican naval attacks on their port cities and to capture all Mexican ships off their coast. If ships were captured, and after prize money was distributed to officers and men, any remaining funds would be split between the two countries.

Moore was also urged to capture Mexican-held cities. If they were on Yucatan-claimed land, they would be turned over to the rebels. If not, Moore could hold them for ransom. After his expenses were deducted, the fleet and the Yucatan government would split the loot.

The Yucatan government agreed to pay the Texas government $8,000 per month for this service. It was an arrangement that would have gladdened the hearts of Henry Morgan, Captain Kidd, or Jean Lafitte. Once again, Moore's proud fleet had a mission.

The Yucatan government urged haste as they learned Mexico was again acquiring a fleet that could outgun and outmaneuver the Texas ships. Mexico had already purchased a Spanish 18-gun brig, and a Mexican agent was in the United States purchasing two schooners to be outfitted for battle. Even worse, Mexican agents were purchasing two large steam-driven ships from British shipyards. With the normal light winds off the Mexican coast, they would be able to outrun and outmaneuver the sail-driven Texas warships.

Lamar was also worried. He rightly feared that after the Mexicans had smashed the Yucatan insurgents, they would turn their formidable land and sea forces against Texas. In spite of the objections of the Sam Houston clique, he ordered Moore to take what ships he could to sea.

The commodore immediately sailed the *San Antonio* to New Orleans to purchase supplies with funds advanced by the Yucatan government. While there, he found a Mexican agent, armed with ample cash, recruiting sailors to man the new Mexican fleet and fight the Texans. To his chagrin, some of those recruited by the Mexican navy were men he had recently laid off.

By December 10, 1841, Moore's provisions and spares had been distributed among the *San Antonio*, *San Bernard*, and the *Austin*.

The following day Moore ordered the *San Antonio* to proceed to the Yucatan port of Sisal to protect the rebel shipping in the area. *San Bernard* was instructed to sweep Mexican merchant ships from the seas between Tampico and Veracruz.

Eighteen forty-one was a Texas presidential election year. Because Lamar was constitutionally unable to succeed himself, he backed Vice President David G. Burnet, who promised to carry out Lamar's policies, against those of a resurgent Sam Houston.

Houston was promising to keep neutral in Mexican politics and to seek a peaceful resolution with Mexico through

Chapter 9

continued negotiations. This was in spite of continual refusal by Mexico to accept Texas as an independent nation. Bad news for the navy, one of his favorite targets, was his pledge of strict economy in government expenses.

Moore on the *Austin* fortunately left Galveston on December 13, the same day that his nemesis, Sam Houston, was again inaugurated president, succeeding Lamar.

One of President Houston's first acts was, on December 15, to send out an order recalling the fleet to Texas. Fortunately, Moore did not receive the written orders until they reached him in the Yucatan in March of 1842.

Houston's next move must be considered more stupid than spiteful. The steamship *Zavala*, the most useful ship in the Texas navy, had continued to rot at anchor since February. Moore needed her badly, but as usual, funds were not available to buy needed parts to keep her engines running or to provision or man her.

Yucatan authorities, acutely aware of the danger from the two Mexican steamships now reportedly heading for the Mexican coast, offered to pay the costs of dry docking the *Zavala*. They agreed to purchase needed parts and to repair, provision, and man her.

Houston curtly refused the offer, and the engines and other key machinery of the *Zavala* continued to rust as the ship, at anchor, began to settle into the sands of Galveston harbor. It was an irreplaceable loss.

On January 5, 1842, Moore's three-ship squadron rendezvoused off Sisal, and the commodore went ashore to confer with Yucatan government officials. What followed was more bizarre than a Marx Brothers comedy.

Moore arrived in Merida, the capital of the Yucatan, on January 10 to find the situation in total turmoil. Peace seemed to be at hand. A Yucatan peace commissioner, Andres Quintana Roo, had reached an agreement with the

Centralist government in Mexico City that would allow the rebellious province to remain in the Mexican fold. And Roo, Moore learned, was even then en route to Mexico City to confirm the agreement.

If the new treaty were ratified, Yucatan instead of being an ally of Texas would become an enemy. Ever brash and on his own initiative, Moore met with the highest officials of the rebel government.

He pointed out to them that if they approved the agreement, it would be tantamount to being at war with Texas and he would act accordingly. His fleet would then dominate the coast, seizing all shipping and blockading all harbors on the peninsula.

In a quick about-face, the Yucatan leaders decided not to act on Roo's peace agreement but instead to continue to negotiate for even better terms with the Central government. Meanwhile, they would continue to pay Moore $8,000 per month. The situation during the next few days was to become even more Byzantine.

While his commodore was facing down the Yucatan government, Lieutenant Alfred G. Gray, in command of the *Austin* in Moore's absence, heard rumors of a Mexico-Yucatan peace treaty. Anchored in Sisal harbor, he observed several longboats filled with well-dressed, distinguished-looking men heading for the schooner *Louisa* anchored nearby. He soon learned that these were Yucatan peace commissioners about to embark on a journey to Veracruz. From there, they would travel overland to Mexico City to sign a peace treaty.

Almost a week had gone by, and Gray had received no communications from the commodore. "The turncoats must have taken him prisoner," he convinced himself. Mulling over the confused situation, Gray conceived a Machiavel-

Chapter 9

lian scheme to free what he thought was his imprisoned commander.

Gray sent a longboat filled with Texas marines to the *Louisa*, boarded her, and took all the peace commissioners prisoner. Amid their outrage and threats, they were taken at gunpoint to the *Austin* and lodged below decks.

When Lt. Gray had sorted them all out, he found that one of the prisoners was no less than Andres Quintana Roo himself, along with half a dozen high-ranking rebel government officials. They were not happy campers on the Texas schooner.

With great courtesy, Gray informed them they would be treated handsomely but would remain on board as hostages until Commodore Moore was released and returned to the *Austin*. Gray released one of the commissioners to carry a message to Moore and the Yucatan government in Merida that he had seized the officials and would hold them until Moore's return.

The freed commissioner, once landed on shore, secured a horse and made the thirty-mile ride to Merida at full speed, arriving at the capital on a foam lathered, exhausted mount in the early hours of the morning. Moore was asleep in his quarters when the breathless messenger gave him the news that his young lieutenant had imprisoned a bevy of Yucatan's most distinguished citizens. It was a rude awakening.

Whether Moore laughed or cried at the news, or whether he was inclined to congratulate his young officer for his initiative or give him fifty lashes for creating a gigantic mess is unknown. But he did dress hurriedly.

He drafted three letters; one to Lt. Gray instructing him to apologize to his prisoners and release them immediately; one to Roo and his fellow commissioners informing them the treaty was in abeyance. The third was a long, humble apology to Yucatan Governor Santiago Mendez for the unauthorized mistake made by a young junior officer. Then he dashed to the governor's mansion to deliver his apology.

In such cases, confusion always runs rampant. While the governor, possibly amused, accepted the apology and dismissed the incident, the word didn't reach the Yucatan foreign minister. That official sent a blistering note of protest both to Moore and to the president of the Republic of Texas.

Shortly afterward the hostages returned to Merida, and amid the general disgruntlement, there were a few good-natured laughs over the incident. On January 22, with the Texas-Yucatan alliance still intact, Moore returned aboard the *Austin*. Then he wrote a long dispatch detailing both his negotiations with the Yucatan government and the unfortunate imprisonment of their peace commissioners.

When Sam Houston read the report, he must have become volcanic.

Moore with the *Austin*, *San Bernard*, and *San Antonio* continued to patrol Mexican coastal waters. On January 24, 1842, the commodore received a desperate message reporting that an American ship, the *Sylph*, had been driven aground by a norther in the Alacranes Islands. Help was needed fast. In response the *Austin* made a hundred-mile sail in rough weather and reached the stricken ship just before she broke up on the reefs.

If the rescue was a dangerous enterprise, the Texans perhaps got a laugh at the name of the wrecked vessel, for she was more like an aging old crone and hardly sylphlike. But the *Austin*'s longboats successfully fought past reefs, through the raging waters and driving winds, to bring off the crew, passengers, and most of the cargo.

Returning to Sisal, Moore transferred the survivors to the *San Antonio*. He ordered Lieutenant William Seeger, the

Chapter 9

schooner's commanding officer, to transport the survivors and his dispatches to his Texas government superiors in Galveston. When the *San Antonio* arrived in Galveston a week later, Seeger first learned of Houston's recall orders, which had not yet reached Moore.

When Seeger delivered his dispatches, the Texas president, in a rage, gave him written orders to return to Sisal and deliver the recall order to Moore. But first, under pressure from the *Sylph*'s owners and passengers, he was ordered to sail to New Orleans and land the shipwreck victims at that port. It was a welcome assignment, for Seeger had Yucatan funds with which to purchase provisions and spares for the other two Texas ships still off the coast of Mexico.

Arriving in New Orleans on February 9, 1842, Seeger anchored the *San Antonio* off the ill-named Slaughterhouse Point rather than taking her alongside a wharf. The anchorage was located in the strong flow of the Mississippi River, and although it was not the most accessible place for provisioning, the distance from land and the strong current made desertion difficult even for strong swimmers.

On February 11, after the survivors of the *Sylph* had been sent ashore, Seeger and his first lieutenant left the ship to make arrangements to purchase supplies. He left the ship in command of young Lieutenant Charles F. Fuller. For fear of mass desertions, the crew was not granted shore leave.

After months at sea, the lights of New Orleans and the nearby port of Algiers beckoned to a crew who longed for the feel of land under their feet. The numerous grog shops and the proffered ministrations of the ladies of New Orleans offered too many temptations to men too long aboard a stinking ship with its lousy food and harsh discipline.

As Lieutenant Fuller stood on the quarterdeck longingly watching the ship's boat depart for the bright lights of the port, the cabin steward, William Barrington, sidled up to him. The steward whispered, "Be careful. There could be trouble," and then slunk off below decks.

All that afternoon and early evening, while the *San Antonio* swayed to her anchor, the bumboats, or harbor traders, came alongside the schooner in their rowboats, canoes, or small sailboats. They peddled fresh fruit, decent bread, unspoiled meat, and forbidden whiskey to men long deprived of these luxuries. "Laundresses" also came out and if slipped aboard, not only washed the sailors filthy, salt-stained clothes, but for a fee supplied other services as well.

As darkness fell, Fuller assigned Sailing Master Monroe H. Dearborn as officer of the deck. He passed on the steward's warning, cautioning Dearborn to look out for trouble. If a nasty situation developed, he was instructed to call out the marine guard. Then Fuller went below to his cabin to get some well-earned rest.

Under cover of darkness, some of the bumboats slipped past the eyes of the officer of the deck, and many bottles of rotgut whiskey were sold to a booze-parched crew, who immediately proceeded to get roaring drunk. Unfortunately, unknown to Dearborn, the most raucous of the whiskey-soaked men were the ship's marines.

By 9 o'clock that night, Dearborn heard loud singing, cursing, and roistering below decks and realized that most of the crew were drunk. He was not particularly worried. He could always call on the marines. These soldiers of the seas had many duties, including sniping from perches in the rigging during battle, leading boarding parties, and providing security for shore parties. Their most important responsibility, however, was to maintain discipline among

Chapter 9

unruly sailors. If the crew got out of hand, he believed, the marines would take care of the trouble.

He was probably not overly concerned when the big, burly, redheaded sergeant of marines, Seymour Oswald, staggered up to the quarterdeck requesting to speak to the officer of the deck.

When Dearborn gave his permission, the sergeant in a slurred voice requested permission to go ashore. Dearborn repeated the captain's orders that shore leave would not be granted. Oswald, in a loud voice, demanded he be given a boat to take him to New Orleans. By this time he was joined by half a dozen sailors clamoring to go ashore.

The noise aroused Fuller, who came on deck as the angry crewmen began to utter threats. The lieutenant turned to Oswald and ordered, "Sergeant, call out the guard."

Oswald saluted, barked a snappy, "Yes Sir," and went below decks. There he issued muskets, bayonets, and cutlasses to two marine corporals and nine privates. He ordered, "Fix bayonets. Lock and load." Then he led his men on deck.

He marched up to Lieutenant Fuller, smiled, and then snarled, "We are going ashore." When the astonished officer remonstrated, Oswald swung at his head with a tomahawk but missed. As Fuller ducked the drunken swing, two of the marines shot him through the body.

As Fuller lay gasping, Corporal Antonio Landois stabbed him, breaking off his bayonet in the dying officer's body.

Midshipmen William H. Allen and Theodore Odell, hearing the shots, rushed to the deck only to be immediately shot down by other marines. The midshipmen along with Dearborn were unceremoniously thrown into a cargo hold and the hatch was locked over them.

Yucatan and a Mutiny

The mutineers now held the ship, but none of them, including Marine Sergeant Oswald, the eleven other marines, Boatswain Frederick Shepherd, a cook, two quartermasters, two stewards including Barrington, and eight other seamen, twenty-six in all, knew how to navigate.

Unlike the infamous mutiny on the *Bounty*, they had no ship's officer to join them. To put out to sea would be like a blind man stumbling along a precipice.

For lack of any other alternative, the men staggered into two ship's boats and rowed toward the bright lights of New Orleans and Algiers where they could find the whisky and whores they craved.

As the boats pulled out, the three officers and the other loyal seamen locked in the hold made a huge racket, banging on the hull and screaming for help. It was not far away.

Officers on the U.S. revenue cutter *Jackson*, anchored nearby and alerted by the musket shots, called out their marine guard and sent them in their longboats in pursuit of the mutineers. One boat rowed to the *San Antonio*, boarded the vessel, released the prisoners, and transported the two wounded midshipmen to shore. They were taken to a New Orleans hospital where they later recovered.

Most of the mutineers, far gone in drunkenness, were captured either by the *Jackson*'s marines or the New Orleans police and promptly thrown in jail. Among those taken were Sergeant Oswald, Corporal Landois, Boatswain Shepherd, and the steward, Barrington. Their fate would be decided later.

In the meantime, while Seeger recruited a new crew and took aboard provisions for the *Austin* and the *San Bernard*, events in Texas overshadowed the problems of the fleet. Texas was again being invaded by Mexican armies.

Chapter 9

A murderous mutiny was quelled aboard the shoal draft schooner *San Antonio* while anchored off the port of New Orleans. Shortly afterward, the ship was lost at sea with all hands during a terrible Gulf storm. (Harry Ransom Humanities Research Center, The University of Texas at Austin)

Chapter 10

Invasion, Betrayal, and a Duel

Eighteen forty-two was to prove to be the most perilous year for the republic since Santa Anna's invasion in 1836. Penny-pinching Houston had disbanded most of the army, and the navy, although recalled, was far away.

Of the naval ships, only the brig *Wharton* and the steamship *Zavala* were in home waters at Galveston. The brig was laid up without crew or provisions, and the steamship was rapidly deteriorating for lack of maintenance and spare parts.

Once again Mexican armies invaded Texas territory, occupying major cities and causing her citizens to flee their homes in terror. A rejuvenated Santa Anna was again in control in Mexico, and he thirsted for revenge against the Texans who had humbled him six years earlier.

In March he sent an army of 700 men, consisting of 400 cavalry, with infantry, artillery, and Indian irregulars under General Rafael Vasquez, across the Rio Grande to spread terror among the undefended settlements.

On March 3 a detachment of 200 men from the Mexican force, under Lt. Col. Ramon Valera, seized Goliad and two

Chapter 10

days later marched into Refugio. Meanwhile, the main body had captured Victoria and then on March 5 captured San Antonio without a battle.

Texan families fled eastward in what was described as another "Runaway Scrape" in which they abandoned homes, stock, and possessions and formed a forlorn procession of refugees streaming toward safety. Women on horseback were seen to cradle babes on their saddles as they fled the advancing Mexican army.

In San Antonio, Vasquez had his men confiscate all wagons and draft animals and then looked the other way while his troops spent two days looting everything of value in the city. Then, with wagons sinking almost up to their axles, he retreated across the Rio Grande.

Houston, having authorized the release of Santa Anna after his capture at San Jacinto, complained:

"Disregarding all the pledges which he had voluntarily made of friendly disposition towards the recognition and establishment of our rights, he evinced upon his resumption of power, the most malignant hostility towards our country and holds out the idea of immediate invasion and molestation."

The Texans feared another invasion was on the way. In his diary of March 11, 1842, William Bollaert, an Englishman visiting in Galveston, wrote:

"It was reported...three Mexican transports were expected off the coast at Paso Caballo [the entrance to Matagorda Bay] with troops, arms and ammunition.... Some of the merchants burnt their goods to save them falling into the hands of the enemy."

And Sam Houston, whose policies had left the country defenseless, fled the new capital at Austin for Galveston.

At that port city, private citizens raised enough money to fit out the brig *Wharton* to sail along the coast and attack Mexican supply ships or troop transports.

In Galveston harbor the only craft readily available for coastal defense was the steamer *Lafitte*. It was operated by a militia unit called the Galveston Coast Guards, which was independent of the regular Texas navy. The ship was manned by enthusiastic volunteers wearing a uniform of red woolen shirts, white trousers, and straw hats.

The guardsmen were accompanied on shipboard by fifty Galveston Fusiliers, another raw, inexperienced but fire-breathing militia unit, equipped with rifles and bayonets. The Coast Guards, according to Bollaert, who was appointed a sergeant of fusiliers, were armed with an assortment of "pikes, boarding swords...hatchets, tomahawks and Bowie knives for close quarters."

On March 14 the *Lafitte*, probably named after the pirate Jean Lafitte, who had once used Galveston as a base for his buccaneering expeditions, steamed over the bar and out into the Gulf on a search for the rumored Mexican men-of-war.

"We had," Bollaert reported, "a fine long brass gun in the bows and two iron carronades on either side and plenty of ammunition."

With ferocious war cries, Bollaert said, "we drilled and exercised with musket and boarding pike. All took to soldiering very kindly but there was a fear that we might kill one another in our anxiety to attack."

On March 17 lookouts spotted what they believed was an enemy schooner attempting to sail over the bar near Matagorda Island.

Shouting "Boarders away," their captain ordered a squad of fusiliers into *Lafitte*'s gig, which was then rowed mightily into the rough water over the bar. Bollaert

Chapter 10

reported, "The breakers were running high; our brave fellows dashed into the foam.... Then they disappeared from our sight and in a few moments the boat was seen bottom up with all hands clinging to her."

"By God, they are swamped," the captain cried. "Man the longboat to rescue our brave fellows," he ordered. As crewmen rushed to launch the boat to attempt a rescue in "dangerous waters," their enthusiasm was suddenly dampened. A lookout in the crow's nest shouted that the crew were "walking in the shoal breakers... while the boat drifted ashore." "However," Bollaert reported, "we gave them three cheers."

On March 18 lookouts spotted the sloop, which had managed to pass over the bar and had proceeded down the coast on inland waters. It had sailed into Aransas Bay where it promptly ran aground. The Texans anchored *Lafitte* off Live Oak Point in the bay and sent the fusiliers to capture the ship.

After a bloodless capture of the ship and a cargo of flour, the fusiliers went ashore on a reconnaissance mission. At a small settlement they met an old settler who told them of the fierce "Koronks," a tribe of cannibals that lived in the area. The old settler told them that the Indians said, "A white man's heart was the sweetest meat they had ever eaten." Aghast, the fusiliers set out to find these demons and spent an entire day forthrightly searching the area. But no "Koronks" being found, they returned to the ship much chagrined.

During the next few days no enemy ships were sighted, but landing parties shot a rattlesnake and a brace of ducks. Sadly for the gung ho fusiliers, these were the only targets they found.

Not dismayed by the lack of enemies to attack, Sergeant Bollaert composed a ballad "Dedicated to the Galveston

Coast Guards" who proudly labeled themselves the "Red Rovers" because of their red woolen shirts.

Anchored in a protected lagoon and filled with "A whiskey punch...claret and segars," the warriors sang the lusty words:

> "Red Rovers, Red Rovers, huzzah!...
> In battle for glory and our bright shining star...
> And the fame of our actions will resound—aye,
>   afar...
> Our cruise being over, our coast free from harm...
> By the girl of his heart...
> The Red Rover is blest."

Having determined there were no enemy ships on the coast, on March 30, accompanied by their captured schooner, the *Lafitte* steamed into Galveston Harbor to be saluted by cannon fire from a local militia company.

"We took only one small prize," Bollaert wrote, "but doubtless had we got a chance, we should have distinguished ourselves."

Considering the puny armament of the *Lafitte*, if they had "gotten their chance" and encountered a Mexican man-of-war, what was a comedy would have quickly become a tragedy.

While the *Lafitte* was safeguarding Texas shores, Houston on March 26 had ordered a blockade of all Mexican ports. In a boastful letter to Santa Anna, Houston threatened:

"In the war which will be conducted by Texas against Mexico...we will march across the Rio Grande, and, believe me, Sir, ere the banner of Mexico shall triumphantly float upon the banks of the Sabine, the Texian standard of the single star...shall display its bright folds in Liberty's triumph, on the isthmus of Darien."

Chapter 10

While mutinies and invasions were taking place on the mainland, the Texas flotilla, sailing in Mexican waters, had not been idle. On February 6, 1842, lookouts on the *Austin* and *San Bernard* spotted the 180-ton schooner *Progreso* leaving Veracruz harbor.

As the *Austin* blocked her seaward movements, the *San Bernard* managed to sail between her and the harbor. Boxed in and with a shot fired across her bow, she struck her colors and heaved to. Since the *Progreso* was found to be carrying a valuable cargo of sugar and flour, Lt. William A. Tennison was put in charge of a prize crew and ordered to sail her to Galveston.

The *Progreso* arrived in that port in mid-February, and ship and cargo were subsequently sold at auction. Although no record of the sale was ever found, her new owner had her sailed to New Orleans. There, after 400 kegs of gunpowder had been loaded aboard her, she hoisted a Mexican flag and set a course for Tampico.

She was an easy prey for the Texas schooners, but for some inexplicable reason, President Houston ordered that the *Progreso* be given a free passage to any Mexican port.

Houston's activities during those days were Machiavellian at best. He was trying to thwart the will of his Congress, who had voted large sums for both the army and the navy. At the same time he was attempting to negotiate with Mexico on the one hand and then on the other was threatening them with blockade and invasion. He was also lying to Moore about supporting the navy. Finally, he was discouraging the mounting pressure from war hawks who wanted to launch a retaliatory invasion of Mexican territory.

Perhaps by giving Mexico safe passage of 400 kegs of gunpowder he was hoping to buy good will. As they said on the Texas-Mexican border, "*Quien sabe?*" Who knows? It was not unlikely, however, that the gunpowder was later fired by General Woll's artillery at Texas militiamen in the ensuing months.

Fortunately Moore was able to collect another $8,000 from Yucatan to partially refit his ships. Another bit of good news was a report that one of the new warships built for the Mexican navy in New York shipyards had been wrecked and sunk in a storm off the Florida Keys. Finally, in late February, the *San Antonio* sailed from New Orleans with a new crew to rejoin Moore and the rest of the flotilla at a rendezvous at the Yucatan port of Laguna.

Arriving at Laguna on March 10, Seeger brought a copy of Houston's order of December 15, 1841, ordering Moore to return with his squadron to Galveston. Seeger may have been aware of the Mexican invasion of Texas and so informed Moore, because the commodore later wrote, "I was compelled by events to disregard that order."

Of more immediate concern, Seeger reported the sad news of the February 11 mutiny aboard the *San Antonio* and the murder of Lt. Fuller. On board the *San Antonio* were two of the thirteen men considered guilty. The others were considered to have been merely drunk. Lt. Seeger had left the remaining eleven in jail in New Orleans.

Anchoring off the Yucatan coast a few days later, Moore had parties fill their kegs with fresh water for the three ships. With that chore completed, he summoned a court-martial board to deal with the two mutineers, Boatswain Frederick Shepherd and Seaman Thomas Rowan. Shepherd, protesting his innocence, asked for a delay until evidence clearing him could be obtained from New Orleans. A stay was approved, and a year later he was found not guilty.

Rowan was not so fortunate. He was convicted and sentenced to be hung. The court, however, recommended

Chapter 10

mercy, and the sentence was changed to 100 lashes with the cat-o-nine tails.

In order to make minor repairs, Moore brought his three ships, the *Austin*, *San Antonio*, and the *San Bernard*, into the small fishing port of Carmen, located at the extreme southwestern end of the Yucatan Peninsula.

With many years of experience at sea, Moore was no novice in suspecting unrest in his ship's crews. In the growing surliness of the men, he detected a scent of mutiny.

Eighteen-year-old Midshipman Edward Johns on board the *Austin* reported that as a precaution Moore ordered all muskets, pistols, and edged weapons be removed from the ship's armory. The weaponry was locked in the officers wardroom under guard.

The following day seaman William Beatts snarled at a petty officer and "made use of mutinous and threatening language." Beatts was immediately clapped in irons and lodged in a rat-infested cell deep in the ship's hold.

Then Moore ordered all hands on all three ships to muster on their foredecks. There, to abashed crews, their captains read the Articles of War with emphasis on the phrases relating to punishment for mutiny. The articles were brief and to the point. The penalty was death by hanging and burial at sea.

Moore, however, realized that the restlessness of his men was a result of their long stay at sea. He decided to grant them shore leave in the little island fishing village of Carmen. It was a remote island set between the Gulf and the Laguna de Terminos. There, he believed, the chances of getting into trouble or deserting were minimal. He was wrong on the first count. When Moore announced to the crews they were to be given shore leave, he was greeted with three rousing cheers.

Invasion, Betrayal, and a Duel

When the first leave parties were selected the afternoon of March 14, sailors from all three ships clambered into their longboats for the two-mile pull from the anchorage to the town. Whether the crewmen had been paid was not recorded, but whatever funds they possessed were spent lavishly.

Carmen was not much to look at, but as a fisherman's port it was studded with waterfront cantinas. There, sloe-eyed ladies in thin, low-cut blouses served a lethal banana brandy to the thirsty seamen. The drink was a specialty of the Mayans who made up the bulk of the population. Banana brandy went down smoothly enough, but after a sufficient amount had gone down the hatch it made one riotously drunk. It didn't take long, and by the evening watch most of the Texans were "three sheets to the wind."

At 5 o'clock that evening a ship's boat hailed the *Austin*, and Midshipman Johns reported that one of the leave party shouted, "The citizens and soldiers of Carmen are murdering our men!" As Lieutenant Cyrus Cummings, the senior officer on board, heard the news, he ordered the ship's cutter lowered. He armed a dozen crewmembers, and he and the men clambered aboard the boat and headed for shore. Shortly after his departure an unknown bumboat passed close to the *Austin*, and someone fired a pistol at Johns. Then the boat slipped away into the darkness.

Meanwhile, Commodore Moore, who was ashore visiting port authorities, was notified of the trouble and rushed to the sleazy waterfront dives. Who started the fighting between the sailors and the local soldiers was never determined. There was, of course, almost always the same pattern for such brawls. Perhaps a drunken Texan pawed a scantily clad bar girl, arousing the envy of the local gallants. It could have started with an argument about cards or claims the sailors were overcharged or a dozen other reasons that seemed important at the time. But there was always the wild and drunken exuberance of men who had been confined on a stinky ship for weeks on end without the sight of a woman or a good strong drink.

When Moore, meeting up with Lieutenant Cummings' detail, reached the waterfront bars, they encountered a scene of sheer bedlam. In the largest establishment, which housed a bar, gambling hall, and whorehouse, all hell was breaking loose. The fighting was taking place in a half-darkened room, where the smoke from native cigars was so thick it looked like one could cut it with a machete. The brawl was a soldiers' and sailors' classic with chairs flung through the air, bottles flying, knives flashing, and curses bellowed in two languages.

As the Texans and the local soldiers pummeled and cut one another, the bar girls fled down the street screaming. Charging into the brawl, Moore got the quick attention of the fighting men, probably by discharging a pistol into the air.

As the melee momentarily paused, Moore announced he would shoot down the next man who started fighting. He talked of mutiny and hanging to calm his men while his threat to burn Carmen to the ground took the fight out of the locals. He ordered Lieutenant Cummings to put three of the crewmen under arrest and march the rest to the docks and have then rowed to their ships.

When a local soldier screamed threats at the Texans, Moore had him arrested and dragged before the local mayor for punishment. Dispersing the mob, the commodore watched his half-drunk, bruised, battered, and cut sailors straggling back to the docks. Then he went to the office of the alcalde and conducted a peace treaty. Moore agreed to prefer no charges against the local soldiers and fishermen if the mayor would forgive all the damages caused by the sailors. There would be, he promised, no more liberty parties inflicted on the town of Carmen. The mayor agreed, probably because the Texans were valued allies. Also, the flotilla's big guns dominated the lagoon.

The following morning, as the hung-over and aching shore party was assembled on the foredecks of the flotilla, two of the men considered instigators of the brawl were stripped and spread-eagled. The *Austin*'s bosun then administered fifty lashes to each man with his cat-o-nine-tails. Perhaps, Moore considered, there would be no more demands for shore leave at Yucatan ports. At least for a while.

On March 31, after repairs were completed and sufficient fresh water taken aboard, the Texas flotilla was sailing off Veracruz when Moore learned that General Vasquez had captured San Antonio. Unknown to him, President Houston on March 26 had issued an order to blockade Mexican ports. It was, of course, a duty Moore had been performing for the past four months. But at last he had been given justification for his actions.

Houston, in one of his confounding changes of policy, had decided to punish the Mexican government for their raid into Texas. He ordered a blockade of the eastern coast of Mexico from Tobasco in the state of Tabasco to Matamoros in the state of Tamaulipas. The blockade included the mouth of the Rio Grande River and all the estuaries, inlets, and passes leading to the Gulf.

The blockade was to exclude the states of Campeche, Yucatan, and Quintana Roo, all of which were in various conditions of revolt against the government in Mexico City. Those provinces were already cooperating closely with the privateers and warships of the Texas navy.

In early April the flotilla was off the Mexican coast and had captured the schooners *Doric*, *Doloritas*, and *Dos*

Chapter 10

Amigos, put prize crews aboard, and sailed them to Galveston.

On April 18, while anchored off Sisal, Moore received news that the agreement with Yucatan had been suspended. The Yucatan government believed that Mexico could not attack them in force for at least a year so they saw no reason to continue to pay Moore his $8,000 a month fee. The Texas ships, however, were free to continue to use Yucatan ports.

On the same day, the brig *Wharton* arrived with Houston's blockade orders. The commodore received additional instructions to return to Galveston to confer with President Houston on naval strategy. Moore ordered the *Austin*, *San Antonio*, and *San Bernard* to proceed to New Orleans for refitting, while, on April 25, he boarded the *Wharton* and prepared to meet with Sam Houston.

On May 1, when Moore arrived in Galveston, he was probably in an optimistic mood. His actions had been finally justified, and Houston apparently realized the necessity for a forward naval strategy.

Meeting with Sam Houston, he was further encouraged by the president after he outlined the bleak condition of his fleet. After more than two years of hard service in tropical waters, the ships were badly in need of extensive repairs and refitting.

Particularly galling was the condition of *Zavala*, the most important ship in the navy. She had so deteriorated that she had to be run aground on a Galveston Bay sandbar to keep her from sinking. Further, *Zavala*'s officers and men had not been paid for months, and Moore feared mass desertion of both sailors and officers.

Houston agreed that the ships should be put in fighting order without delay, that a vigorous blockade should again be launched against Mexican ports, and that Mexican shipping should be driven from the Gulf.

Elated, Moore returned to Galveston, promised his disaffected men they would be paid, then boarded the *Austin* for a hurried trip to New Orleans to supervise the refitting of his ships.

As the *Wharton* rocked at anchor in New Orleans while Moore was busy ashore, idle midshipmen in crowded quarters were stewing with adolescent disputes. Their quarrels usually had little substance but were a combination of hot tempers, idleness, frustration, and the lethal Southern sense of honor.

Over some trivial slight, real or imagined, Midshipman George W. White challenged Midshipman Fielding R. Culp to a duel. Their belligerence was undoubtedly aroused by a combination of hot humid nights and too much time to brood over their usually wretched living conditions. There was also, of course, the Southern gentlemen's capacity for instant violence that often resulted in brawls, duels, and feuds, which in retrospect could have been resolved peaceably over time and with cooler heads.

Naval officers were particularly prone to dueling if their personal honor or integrity was impugned. Sadly, most of the older officers in the service were of little help in dissuading duels since many believed such fighting fostered both courage among men and courtesy between officers.

Custom decreed that such encounters in New Orleans should be settled at the Dueling Oaks. The oaks were located in a park a few miles south of Lake Pontchartrain where the gnarled trees cast ominous shadows upon deadly contests held at dawn.

During first light on the morning following the challenge, the two midshipmen, their appointed seconds, a judge, and the ship's doctor were rowed ashore and taken to the Dueling Oaks by carriage. There would, tradition said, be breakfast for one and death for the other.

Based on the ancient Irish Code Duello, the fight was to be a formal affair. The seconds greeted each other politely and then approached each of the men requesting a reconciliation. This refused, the two dueling weapons, often .44-caliber percussion pistols, finely engraved and perfectly balanced, were presented. The weapons lay in a polished mahogany or walnut box, and each man chose his pistol.

Also inside the box were matching lead balls, percussion caps, and a priming powder flask. After the weapons were loaded by the seconds, the principals stood facing one another at an agreed distance.

The pistols were cocked and held upright by each duelist. When the judge gave the command, "Fire," the men extended their arms toward their opponent and pulled the triggers. Deliberate aiming was considered ungentlemanly. One fired when his weapon lined up with the opponent as the arm descended.

Depending on the distance, there could be many misses by both shooters. In those cases, pistols were reloaded and the men continued to fire until it was agreed that honor had been satisfied or one or both duelists were badly or mortally wounded.

In the duel between White and Culp, the latter fell mortally wounded after the first exchange.

In another affair of honor, Midshipman Peyton Middleton and Midshipman C.L. Faysoux felt compelled to try to kill one another.

As the sun first peeked over the grim oak trees, the two, both known to be expert pistol shots, prepared to fire at one another. George F. Fuller, another midshipman aboard the *Wharton*, described the event:

"Faysoux fired first as Middleton was coolly and carefully lowering his pistol to the mark. The bullet from Faysoux's pistol struck the hammer of his adversary's weapon and glancing from that shattered Middleton's cheekbone.

"As the bullet struck the lock it caused a premature discharge of Middleton's pistol, and the bullet thus hastened by the fifth of a second, struck the rim of Faysoux's cap and came out the top of it. Faysoux told me that he felt the bullet pass over the hair of his head."

Honor thus satisfied, Middleton was treated by the doctor for a shattered face while Faysoux journeyed to New Orleans to purchase a new hat.

Meanwhile, Moore was quickly disillusioned of belief in Houston's promises. Instead of providing cash, the president had only issued notes promising to pay bills at some unspecified date. This was anathema to the New Orleans ship fitters, who refused further credit.

Moore, in an agony of frustration, returned to Austin, bypassed Sam Houston, and appealed directly to the legislature for funds. The Texas Congress, fearful of another Mexican invasion, voted almost $98,000 for refitting the navy ships. But again Houston outwitted his belligerent legislators and would only issue promissory notes instead of cash.

At this, Moore exploded and confronted Houston. In a roaring tirade he issued an ultimatum in which he threatened to "Disband the navy and leave it to rot in a foreign port."

"You are," the commodore yelled, "a humbug and I will not be humbugged by you any more." Houston was noted for a violent temper and at six feet, three inches tall, was a giant of a man for those times. The president towered over

Chapter 10

his five-foot, eight-inch subordinate, but surprisingly, he remained cool under Moore's tirade.

Soothingly, Houston promised he would issue funds immediately. The following day, Moore received not the $98,000 but $18,812 in Exchequer bills, which were redeemable in cash. He was also given sealed orders to be opened when he reached New Orleans.

Moore, buoyed by even this small infusion of funds, returned to New Orleans and opened his sealed orders, expecting they would contain instructions for leading the fleet to Mexican waters.

Instead, Houston forbade him to spend the Exchequer bills and ordered that he use them only as collateral for loans from naval outfitters who would agree to extend credit for an indefinite period of time. The bills, Moore calculated, would be worth only twenty-five cents on the dollar, if indeed he could find any merchant who would accept them.

There were other disasters. The *Zavala*, by now rotted beyond repair, sank on the sandbar in Galveston harbor. The *San Bernard*, with a hull worm-eaten and rotten, tried to make it to New Orleans for the limited repairs that Moore could afford but was hit by a storm, driven ashore, and badly smashed up.

In a desperate effort to acquire funds, Moore asked the gallant Lt. Seeger to try to sail the leaky *San Antonio* to Sisal and beg for money. Seeger said he would give it a try, and in August he sailed for the Yucatan. He and the schooner were never heard from again. Apparently the *San Antonio* fell prey to one of the fierce storms that often ripped across the Gulf during the late summer months. The lieutenant and his crew paid the final price for Houston's double-cross.

In an attempt to punish Mexico for their invasion of Texas soil and the looting of San Antonio, the Texas House

Invasion, Betrayal, and a Duel

The Texas navy's steamship *Zavala* was the most powerful ship in the fleet. After surviving a ferocious storm, starved of funds for repairs, it rotted and sank in Galveston Harbor. (Courtesy of the Rosenberg Library, Galveston, Texas)

of Representatives passed a bill calling for an invasion of that country. On July 22, 1842, Houston repudiated their action, writing to the House that:

"If Mexico is invaded, it must be by a force, whose term of service will not be less than one year and whose numbers should not be less than five thousand men.... Six months would be necessary to perfect them in the manual exercise, the drill and the duties of the camp. No time would be afforded for operations against the enemy. As soon as the time for which they were engaged would expire, if they were not discharged, discontent and mutiny would arise, with a breaking up to finish the catastrophe. Five thousand

Chapter 10

men returning to the settlements of Texas, disorganized and exasperated, would be more formidable than four times their number of the enemy."

Most Texans, however, were more concerned about an invading Mexican army than they would be about their demobilized neighbors. As a further caveat, Houston stated that the proposed invasion would cost at least $2 million. The Texas treasury, he added, was virtually empty.

As an afterthought, he stated there were no funds available for the Texas navy to "take possession of the Gulf against the Mexican navy. Months and perhaps years must elapse before the resources are...available for fitting out the Navy," he said.

Houston, however, did not reckon with the determination of Commodore Edwin Ward Moore.

If the *San Antonio* had completed her mission, she may have indeed returned with ample funds for the Texas navy because Santa Anna, with new ships, was on the attack. A Mexican squadron had already sunk one of the only two brigs in the Yucatan navy, and two Mexican armies were preparing to advance on Campeche and Merida.

At the same time, General Adrian Woll was preparing to launch another major attack on Texas.

Chapter 11

A New Monster Threatens

Crushing the Republic of Texas was the burning passion of Santa Anna. In August 1842 he instructed General Adrian Woll, a French mercenary soldier commanding the Second Division of the Mexican Army Corps of the North, to prepare for an attack on San Antonio. On August 24 Woll's army of more than 1,000 men assembled at Presidio del Rio Grande and began its 125-mile march to the city. It was an impressive force for that day and included 600 cavalry and 400 infantry. There were two artillery pieces and an artillery train. To supply the army there were 12 wagons loaded with corn, 150 wagons with other provisions, and 50 head of cattle. The expedition also consisted of 919 horses and 213 mules.

Woll, no slouch at histrionics, addressed his troops announcing the "second campaign against Texas," and promised them:

"Victory will crown your heroic efforts and a generous country will reward your worthiness. Soldiers, let us march then upon the enemy."

Chapter 11

On the night of September 10, the Mexican force reached San Antonio and surrounded the town, cutting off all roads. The next morning only sporadic resistance was offered by the 100 Tejanos and 75 Anglo citizen volunteers, who were quickly brushed aside when Woll opened up with his 4-pounder and 6-pounder cannon.

To the accompaniment of a military band playing the dancing tune "La Cachucha," the Mexican army marched into the city plaza, hauled down the Lone Star flag, and replaced it with the Mexican tricolor. Back in Austin on the previous day, the gullible Houston had cancelled his orders to blockade Mexican ports.

Woll took sixty-two Anglo prisoners in San Antonio and had them marched into Mexico, where they languished in jail until their release many months later.

While the Mexican general's troops were 150 miles deep into Texas territory, on September 12, 1842, Houston had revoked the blockade of Mexican ports. His reasoning, he later explained to the Congress, was that the British government was complaining that Texas warships were seizing their merchantmen unlawfully.

Also, after long negotiations, Texas had finally concluded a "treaty of recognition, friendship and commerce" with the British. In response for their recognition, Houston called off the Texas warships. He continually held the vain and unwarranted hope that the British would pressure Santa Anna into concluding a peace treaty with Texas.

To this end he made continued plaintive requests to Captain Charles Elliott, the British representative in Austin, asking for his intercession with the Mexican dictator. He pointed out, "It was the duty of England, under a solemn treaty to offer mediation."

But as he finally admitted to the Texas Congress, "So far their efforts have been rejected."

A New Monster Threatens

On September 18, after a skirmish at Salado Creek against 300 unorganized Texas volunteers, Woll withdrew his men back to San Antonio. Two days later, after holding the town for ten days, he ordered a general withdrawal across the Rio Grande.

As the Mexican army left, they confiscated all wagons, horses, and mules, including 500 head of cattle. There was some discontent among the troops as there was not much left to loot in the town after General Vasquez's plundering raid only six months earlier. After several skirmishes with pursuing Texans, Woll's army crossed back into Mexico on October 1.

Although these Mexican incursions have been dismissed as mere raids by many historians and partisans of the Houston myth, they had a disastrous effect on the young republic. The raids weakened Texas's claim to sovereignty as they demonstrated that the government could not protect its borders or its people from invading Mexican armies.

The raids not only discouraged immigration into the frontier settlements, but also ruined farmers and businessmen from the Rio Grande to San Antonio who had their possessions either stolen or burned.

Agriculture was curtailed as Texas farmers fled to the east with their families or took up their rifles and marched with improvised militia. While crops lay rotting on the ground, one Texan wrote, "Those sections of the country trembling under the battle axe of the enemy will not pay taxes or produce crops."

The constant turmoil also discouraged Houston's dream of the annexation of Texas by the United States as many of the Congress of that country had no desire to become embroiled in a military confrontation with Mexico. That would come later.

Chapter 11

But as Woll retreated, an even more dangerous threat to Texas was rapidly developing. For while Mexico stalled Houston's overtures for peace, the few funds available for refitting Moore's ships were frittered away. All the while a monster was growing in Mexican waters.

The two modern steam-driven warships built in British shipyards for the Mexican navy had been delivered to Veracruz. The *Guadalupe* was the first steam-driven, twin paddle-wheeled, iron hulled warship ever built and was powered by two 180 horsepower engines. She featured watertight bulkheads, improved internal stowage capacity, and the ability of iron plating to endure gunfire without the splintering of wood. She displaced 775 tons, but with a shallow draft of only ten feet she was ideal to operate in the shoal waters of the Gulf of Mexico.

With improved swivel gun mounts, the *Guadalupe* was armed with new Paixhan shell guns consisting of two long, monstrous 68-pounders and four 12-pounders. She was at the cutting edge of nautical technology, both in propulsion and gunnery. With experienced British naval officers at the helm, she alone was more than a match for the entire Texas navy. One British gunner described the 68-pounder shells as "large as pumpkins."

The other British-built warship, the *Moctezuma*, was of wooden construction and weighed in at a monstrous 1,100 tons. She was propelled by two 280 horsepower steam engines driving two paddle wheels. The warship carried a massive Paixhan battery of two 68-pounders on swivel mounts, two long range 32-pounders, four 32-pounder short range carronades, and a 9-pounder. She too had sufficient firepower to whip the entire Texas fleet.

The Mexican government hired experienced British naval gunners to man the batteries of their two steam-driven warships. Their officers were on long leaves of absence from the Royal navy.

A third steamer, the *Regenerador*, was a well-armed converted merchantman. In addition, the Mexican sailing ships were themselves more than a match for the Texans. They consisted of two brigs, the *Yucateo* and the *Iman*, and the armed schooners *Aguila* and *Campechano*.

During the late fall and winter of 1842, Commodore Moore, vainly hoping for additional funds, used his own credit with New Orleans ship fitters to keep the *Austin* and the *Wharton*, his sole remaining ships, battle ready.

A final plea to the Yucatan government, now hard pressed by Mexican forces, brought him an additional $7,000 in cash. With these funds put to use, by early 1843 Moore was ready to take his ships to sea and play David to the Mexican Goliath.

But again the devious Houston had been encouraged by a British naval captain to believe that a diplomatic success with Mexico was near. The British government had a two-fold reason for weakening the Texas navy. First, Moore's blockading tactics, like those of the earlier Texas privateers, had crippled their lucrative trade with Mexico.

Secondly, they wanted Texas dependent on British goodwill. What they did not want was a strong republic, which, if annexed by the United States, would dominate the trade of the Gulf of Mexico and probably the entire Caribbean.

To advance these ends they had allowed the two massive warships to be built in British shipyards and then winked at British naval officers joining the Mexican navy.

Pursuing these policies, British diplomats convinced Houston that they could mediate a peace treaty between Texas and Mexico only if the blockade of Mexican ports was ended.

Although Texas agents in London had protested the construction of the Mexican warships and their manning by British officers, they were stalled and rebuffed by the British Foreign Office. While British officials protested they held no animosities against the new republic, it was obvious they were only interested in the continuation of their profitable mercantile relationship with Mexico.

In a message to the Texas Congress on December 22, 1842, Houston complained that the Texas navy would cost $300,000 to maintain, and that this expense:

"Requires us to abandon that arm of defense, and make sale or such other disposition of the vessels as will relieve the nation from a burthen [sic] which it is so utterly unable to sustain."

Demonstrating less than an elephantine memory, he wrote of the navy:

"When we advert to the history of our Navy from its first establishment to the present moment, we can not perceive a single instance wherein any important benefit has been conferred upon the country from its action. No advantage has been achieved. This remark has not been made from any disposition to reflect any disparagement upon the officers composing the naval corps, but is founded upon facts which are to be deplored, because they have encumbered us with debt, without producing any beneficial return."

Inanely, he suggested that the funds "wasted" on the Texas navy should have been used to construct coastal defenses and fortifications for harbors. However, he appropriated no funds for such projects. Moreover, it was of dubious probability that coastal defenses, even if properly constructed and manned, could keep an enemy out of Texas harbors. Even if successful, harbor defenses would not have prevented a blockade by the Mexican navy from strangling all seaborne trade to and from the new republic.

Houston reported to the Texas Congress that Moore was incompetent, had squandered his appropriations (which he had never received), and was unable to take his ships to sea.

On January 10, 1843, Houston made an alarming announcement to Congress, writing:

"Mexico, in the event of being successful against Yucatan will immediately invade Texas with a formidable force by land and sea.... It will be attempted during the ensuing spring.... It may be supposed, that all her available energies will be called into action."

The Texas president exhorted, "Every means in our power should be called into action and be in readiness for any event."

To meet this threat, Houston complained:

"At this time we have no organized force. We have no ammunition, and our arms are in bad order.... There is not now a single pound of lead, nor a single keg of rifle powder in possession of the government for the public defense....

"We have yet time to organize our forces...so as to meet and to counteract the probable movements of the enemy. This may be done at an expense not exceeding two thousand dollars."

As a military strategist, Houston proposed an army of infantry to fight on the plains of Texas. He stated there should be, "Few cavalry because...their [the soldiers'] attention will necessarily be called to the care of their horses. A neglect of duty, great confusion and increase of labor will be the consequence."

His proposed tactics were at variance with those of a Texas congressman who remarked that infantry units stationed in the wide open spaces of the state were "as useful as lobsters."

Houston's letter continued:

Chapter 11

"If Texas is invaded, the object will certainly be to overrun the country by a formidable force.... [The Mexicans would] have the entire command of our waters, and the gulf, and could sustain themselves, receiving supplies by water."

According to Houston's strategy, scattered militia forces would be raised and assembled at a minute cost. Untrained and virtually unorganized, they would then take their squirrel guns from the mantelpiece and march out to defeat a large Mexican regular army.

Expanding on his strategy, in his December 22 missive, Houston stated that he:

"Anticipates confidently a treaty of peace and amity with all the Indians upon our borders... with small encouragement [they will] deprive the enemy of their cavalry and pack horses.... And whilst the Indians would be thus employed, they would not be permitted to violate any principle or law of humanity."

He concluded that the Indian tribes would have "a zeal for our service." He did not explain how during this fantastical alliance he would prevent his allies of Apache, Comanche, Kiowa, and Kickapoos from indulging in their raiding pleasures. These included rape, scalping, roasting heads over slow fires, amputating genitals and stuffing them in the mouths of victims, gouging out eyes, and other amusing pleasures those tribes performed on prisoners.

He also asked the Congress to make him the supreme commander of all the fighting forces of Texas, in effect a military dictator.

Houston conceded that Mexican warships would dominate the Texas coastline and would therefore be able to supply and reinforce their armies at will.

Apparently, to make certain this disaster would occur, six days later, on January 16, Houston persuaded a tame

A New Monster Threatens

and confused Congress to pass a legislative act providing for the sale of all the remaining ships of the Texas navy. Not only did the act authorize Texas government agents, "To dispose of the vessels of the navy," but it also provided for the sale of the Galveston navy yard and all its stores. This, of course, would make it impossible to quickly reconstitute a naval force.

Unknown to Houston, Commodore Moore, in New Orleans, was frantically trying to get shipyard bills paid so he could take his squadron to sea. On January 17, the day after Houston got approval from Congress to sell the navy, Moore dispatched the schooner *Two Sons* to Yucatan with a plea for funds.

He asked for $20,000 in cash and $8,000 per month thereafter. He promised he would drive the Mexican fleet from Yucatan waters. By fulfilling this promise, he said, he would win the war for the revolutionaries.

The distance from Mexico City to the Yucatan capital of Merida by land was more than 750 miles over a route that was more trails than roads. Consequently, the two Mexican armies attempting to suppress the revolt were supplied by their fleet. If Moore captured, sunk, or drove off Mexican supply ships, the Mexican armies would soon be forced to retreat.

The Yucatan authorities were enthusiastic about Texan intervention, and by February 11, 1843, Colonel Martin Peraza arrived in New Orleans with a down payment of more than $7,000 in cash. On February 25, however, Moore found that the wily president of Texas had taken further steps to insure the destruction of the Texas navy. On that date he was confronted by two newly appointed naval commissioners, Colonel James Morgan and William Bryan.

During the Texas Revolution, Morgan, a prosperous businessman with shipping and real estate interests, was

Chapter 11

appointed a colonel in the Texas army. During 1836 he became commandant of Galveston Island and planned and had built the fortifications on that island. Although Houston accused him of incompetence in designing Galveston's defenses, he nevertheless appointed him navy commissioner in 1843.

Bryan was a former New Orleans merchant. After coming to Texas in 1836, he was appointed Texas consul in New Orleans by President Mirabeau B. Lamar. Early in 1842 he returned to Texas where he remained in business until he received the Houston appointment.

Houston had given the men strict instructions:

"I now render my orders...in passing the Secret act for the disposition of the Navy.... Proceed to New Orleans... employ all proper and legal means to get possession of the ship *Austin* and the brig *Wharton*, likewise all the public stores, arms, equipment, and public property."

He instructed them that, "Should any resistance be made" they were to request that the United States government force compliance. Houston's dictate continued:

"Post Captain E.W. Moore has had no authority from this Government, to ship men, appoint officers, enlist marines, or do any other act, or thing, but to sail to the port of Galveston, and report or turn over the command of the navy to the senior officer present and then report in person to the Navy Department. Since the 29th October 1842, he has had no authority to enter into any arrangements with Yucatan, nor could do so, without contumacy to his superiors, or treason to his country.

"The fact of his shipping men, or enlisting or receiving, volunteer marines, with an intention of going out to sea, without the orders, or sanction of his government, on armed vessels, will clearly render it a case cognizable by the government authorities of the United States. His defiance of the laws of his own country to which he owes allegiance is clearly treason.

"Not to obey his orders is unofficerlike, to resist them is mutiny and to defy them is treason. For him to persist would be piracy. Should Post Captain E.W. Moore not forthwith render obedience to the orders of the department, you will have published, in one or more newspapers in the city of New Orleans my Proclamation.

"Our national humiliation is attributable to a few disorganizing men, who seek power without merit, and a few incendiary presses, which are supported by such men, with the avowed design, of prostrating the constitutional officers by revolution. They shall fail."

Houston's motives are difficult, if not impossible, to fathom. Were his actions motivated by a desire to establish a tighter grip on his Congress? Was he drunk? Confused? Did he actually believe in the benevolence of the British government? What made him think that Santa Anna was willing to recognize the independence of Texas? Perhaps a clue to his motives can be found in his suggestion to Congress that in the event of a Mexican invasion, he should be given personal command of the army with unlimited powers. He would then be not only a constitutional president, but a military dictator.

Winston Churchill once remarked of the Russians that they were, "A riddle wrapped in a mystery inside an enigma." The same might be said of Sam Houston.

The *New Orleans Tropic* newspaper put it more bluntly:

"If the next arrival from Texas does not inform us that the miserable fool who presides over the fate of Texas at the present time has been lynched, we shall be disappointed."

Samuel Swartwout, the New York financier who in 1836 had bailed out the *Invincible* and the *Brutus* when they were unable to sail until a shipyard was paid an overdue repair

Chapter 11

bill, put it more simply. In a letter to Commissioner Morgan he wrote, "Houston is mad."

After arriving in New Orleans and talking with Moore, the two commissioners began to have second thoughts about selling the navy. They had been given broad discretionary powers by the Texas Seventh Congress to act as they saw fit for the benefit of Texas.

Concerned, they wrote the Texas secretaries of War and Navy, describing their conversations with Moore and asked for advice and counsel. On April 4 they received their answer. The fine hand of Sam Houston was evident in the document, which stated that Moore was relieved of command. The commodore was ordered to immediately leave New Orleans and report to his superiors in Austin under arrest. All previous orders were rescinded.

Outrageously, there was appended a secret document to be used only if Moore disobeyed orders and sailed to the rescue of Yucatan. It stated that Moore and his officers and crews were to be considered pirates. Ships of all nations were authorized to capture the *Austin* and *Wharton* and bring the ships and crews to Galveston. There, Moore would be tried for piracy. Presumably Houston would then have the perverse satisfaction of seeing the commodore of the Texas navy dancing from a gibbet.

Moore retained his composure after the shock of these orders. He convinced the commissioners that he should sail his two ships to Galveston where he would then report to the authorities. He told Morgan and Bryan that if he abandoned his ships in New Orleans, "The officers will resign." He said his unpaid sailors had threatened that if they did not receive the pay due them they "would mutiny and destroy the ships."

Sam Houston was totally ignorant of the strategic necessity for sea power. A vindictive man, he attempted to destroy the Texas navy and disgrace its officers. He declared Commodore Moore's squadron to be "pirates." (Texas State Library and Archives Commission)

The commissioners agreed and Moore, commanding his two remaining ships and accompanied by Colonel Morgan, prepared to sail to Galveston.

On April 18 the flotilla was anchored in the mouth of the Mississippi while waiting for fog to lift so they could sail into the Gulf. The following day they received frightening news. The Yucatan ship *Rosario*, fresh out of Campeche, dropped anchor nearby and her captain went aboard the *Austin*.

Chapter 11

He informed the Texans that under the big guns of the Mexican fleet and savage assaults by the army, Yucatan resistance was collapsing. The *Rosario*'s captain reported that Campeche was being bombarded by a Mexican fleet composed of the three steamers, five sailing ships, and a number of transports. The fleet, he said, had landed 8,000 Mexican soldiers who were preparing to assault the city walls after the giant Paixhan guns had smashed them to rubble.

Many of the Mexican troops had been transported from Matamoros to the beaches of Campeche by chartered American merchant ships out of New Orleans. The Texas navy, the captain said, would have to act fast to save the Yucatan.

If they failed, the powerful Mexican navy would be free to carry out Santa Anna's plans for reconquering Texas. The captain reported that the Mexican fleet, accompanied by transports loaded with 6,000 troops, was preparing to attack Galveston.

If Moore was concerned, Colonel Morgan panicked. He later wrote he would use his discretionary powers to overrule Houston and "save the Republic if I could."

In effect, he said to hell with the president of the Republic of Texas, and he ordered the Texas fleet to sea. He, as Secretary of the Navy Fisher had done, put his country before his career and disobeyed his orders. He later wrote, "Our vessels were in apple pie order... the officers anxious [to fight]... knowing if our vessels did go into Galveston Harbor they would never come out again as Texas ships.... Considering the officers had never received one cent of pay for the last two years—if the navy was sold they never would [be paid].... Now an opportunity offered to do something for... their adopted country.... I concluded to stretch my authority as Commissioner and authorize Commodore Moore to go ahead."

Moore, outraged at a possible charge of piracy, wrote to Texas authorities, stating:

"In the event of my being declared... by the President as a pirate or outlaw; please state... I go down to attack the Mexican squadron, with the consent and full concurrence of Colonel James Morgan... who is going with me, believing as he does that it is the best thing that can be done for the country. This ship and brig have excellent men... and the officers and men... are eager for the contest. We go to make one desperate struggle to turn the tide of ill luck."

Moore fudged a bit on the "excellence" of some of his crew. Earlier, unpaid Texas navy sailors had threatened to burn their ships if their pay was not forthcoming. The Yucatan funds relieved this crisis, but their anger was not an aid to recruiting good men. In addition, the U.S. Navy was recruiting in New Orleans, offering hard cash to experienced seamen.

To fill out his crews, Moore was forced to take more than forty men from the city's jails. Moore needed bodies, and New Orleans authorities were happy to get rid of several dozens of drunks and miscreants.

On April 19, 1843, amidst the cheers of the crew, Commissioner Morgan gave Moore authority to sail to the Yucatan. "On a moonless night, as black as a crow's wing," the *Austin* and the *Wharton* sailed out of New Orleans on a mission to fight the mighty Mexican warships.

But first there was some unfinished business to be resolved. Before departing, Moore had the mutineers of the *San Antonio* taken from the New Orleans jail and put in irons aboard the *Austin*. When they got to sea a court-martial was convened, a trial conducted, and sentences handed down.

The trials were handicapped since the *San Antonio*, with many of the witnesses, had gone down with all hands in

Chapter 11

September while the mutineers were still in jail in New Orleans. Boatswain Shepherd, however, agreed to testify against the other mutineers. For this, and because evidence indicated he was probably innocent, he was acquitted. The court-martial board sentenced the less culpable to the lash. Seaman Thomas F. Rowan was sentenced to receive 50 lashes with a cat-of-nine-tails while Cabin Steward William Barrington and the ship's cook, Edward Keener, each were to receive 100 lashes.

Those implicated in the murder of Lieutenant Fuller, however, would pay with their lives. Marine Corporal William Simpson and Marine Private Antonio Landois, who had plunged his bayonet into the dying Fuller, as well as Seamen James Hudgins and Boatswain Issac Allen were sentenced to be hanged.

Marine Private Benjamin Pompilly escaped the noose by dying in jail, and the chief instigator and leader of the mutineers, Marine Sergeant Seymour Oswald, managed to escape from the prison the day before he was to be transferred to the *Austin*. He was never found.

On April 26 the flagship hove to in order to carry out punishment. The crew and the prisoners were assembled on deck and in a deathly quiet, Moore addressed his men, reading out the sentences.

He told them that he hated executions and had never had to do this fearsome duty before and "I hope to God I never have to do it again." But he reminded them that the convicted men had not only committed mutiny but had in cold blood murdered Lt. Fuller and wounded two midshipmen. The sentences were reached after a fair trial, he said, and they would be carried out the following day. He told the condemned to prepare to meet their God and then dismissed the crew.

A New Monster Threatens

At high noon, April 26, all hands were assembled to witness punishment as the officers, wearing side arms, stood on the quarterdeck.

It was then that the boatswain informed the officiating officer, Lt. Alfred G. Gray, that he did not know how to tie a hangman's knot. When Gray queried the crew, asking for a volunteer who knew how to tie the knots, all shook their heads.

Gray snorted in disgust at what was obviously a pack of lies and grumbled, "I'll tie the damned things myself." That chore completed, the ceremony began. Midshipman Fuller described the events:

"Four lines were suspended from the foreyard after the foresail had been furled. Then the four lines from the weather and lee yardarms were led through blocks on the deck and were 'married' together. They were then passed through leading blocks aft to and around the main mast and forward to a point under the yard.

"One half of the crew were to walk aft with the line, the other half to walk forward."

In navy style hangings the men were not dropped but hoisted.

Midshipman Fuller later wrote:

"The prisoners were brought forth and the ropes were passed around their necks. The Commodore gave the signal, a shot from the bow gun, and the crew started on their death march. The four culprits were raised to the yard arm and must have strangled in the ascent; for they neither struggled nor made the slightest motion."

The bodies were left hanging at the foreyard for an hour. Then they were taken down, and the ship's surgeon read a funeral service over them. Their bodies were sewn in a canvas shroud with a cannon ball at their feet and then they were launched over the side and into the Gulf.

Chapter 11

On the following day the crew was again assembled to witness the punishment of the more fortunate mutineers. Midshipman Fuller reported:

"Barrington was served up at the gangway, naked to the waist. The boatswain gave the first blow with the 'cat,' with its nine cords; a reddish tinge appeared as the cat was raised for the second stroke; the marks on the back assumed, as the punishment continued, a purple hue, then the blood flowed.

"The surgeon stood by with his hand on the culprit's wrist. At the end of 50 lashes he made a sign that signified, 'This man can bear no more,' which caused his release. A shirt was thrown over his back, and he was led forward. He did not, at any time afterward, receive the other fifty lashes."

The other mutineers, at Moore's orders, received only fifty lashes. Perhaps the commodore believed the message delivered to the crew was sufficient.

Following the punishments, the boatswain piped the sailors aloft to set all sails while Moore set a course for Yucatan waters. From information gleaned from Yucatan coasters, Moore learned that the *Montezuma* was anchored in the northern Yucatan port of Telchac, 150 miles north of besieged Campeche.

Hoping to catch and defeat the Mexican steamer before other units of the Mexican fleet could come to her aid, Moore bent on all sails for the Yucatan port. Twice a day all hands were piped to battle stations to practice gunnery. The Texans reached Telchac on April 27 only to learn the *Montezuma* had departed on the 26th.

Racing after her, the Texas flotilla was offshore at the port of Lerma on April 29 when a lookout sighted the entire Mexican fleet ten miles south of the harbor. The showdown, Moore thought, had come at last.

Chapter 12

Battle at Sea

It was almost twilight when both Texas ships beat to quarters and cleared for action. Commodore Moore stood on the quarterdeck in his best uniform and pledged to his crew that if the battle was lost, there would be no surrender. He would not languish in a Mexican prison waiting to be executed by Santa Anna.

He would, he said, "put a match to the powder magazine" and send himself and the *Austin* to Davy Jones' locker. At this, his crew gave three cheers and swore they would fight to the end. Then darkness fell and the tropical night shrouded the waters like a blanket. Moore impatiently postponed his attack until dawn. During a long night the two fleets maneuvered for position until they were both in waters approximately fifteen miles northwest of Lerma.

Midshipman Alfred Walke, aboard the *Austin*, wrote in his logbook:

"Sunday, April 30, 1843. At 4:45 as day broke the enemy hove in sight consisting of the steamers *Montezuma* and *Guadalupe*, brig *Yucatan* and the schooners *Eagle, Iman,* and *Campechano.*"

Chapter 12

Midshipman Fuller aboard the *Austin* wrote, "We were under the three topsails, jib and spenser... at six knots in a light breeze... and the enemy... were slightly to windward."

At this time, the lookout spotted the Yucatan squadron, commanded by the redoubtable Captain James Boylan, coming up astern. The squadron was small but game. It consisted of the small schooners *Siselano* and *Independencia* armed with long 18-pounders, followed by five lightly armed pirogues or canoas, each carrying one 6-pounder.

By 7 o'clock, when the morning mist cleared, the Mexican fleet with the exception of the flagship *Guadalupe* hoisted the Mexican national flag. That ship was commanded by Captain E.P. Charlewood, on leave from the British navy, and his crew, mostly Englishmen, insisted on flying the British Union Jack at the masthead. In response, Moore's ships hoisted the Texas Lone Star ensign to the peak of their mainmasts as the crews cheered.

Badly outnumbered and greatly outgunned, the Texans prepared to attack. It was not only rash, some might have called it suicidal, but Moore in the tradition of American naval officers since John Paul Jones was eager to put his ships in harm's way.

The firepower of the Mexican fleet was horrendous. The *Montezuma* and *Guadalupe* mounted four monstrous 68-pounders, six 32-pounders, four 12-pounders, and a 9-pounder. These guns alone could turn the Texans and their Yucatan allies into splintered wrecks in short order. But in addition, their sailing ships mounted one 32-pounder, twenty-three 18-pounders, one 12-pounder, and eight 6-pounders. Many of their guns were Paixhans and not only outranged the Texas but threw heavier and more explosive shells.

The Texans could muster only sixteen 24-pounders, nineteen 18-pounders, and one 9-pounder. Moreover, Moore's two ships were manned by less than half their full complement of men. The *Austin* had a crew of 146 and the *Wharton* only 86. If they were few in numbers, they made up for it in toughness. Some of the ship's boys who hauled gunpowder up on deck from the *Austin*'s magazine were less than teenagers. Midshipman Fairfax Gray, who commanded the battery of two guns positioned in the commodore's cabin, was only fourteen years old.

As they went into battle, Commissioner Morgan later commented:

"Commodore Moore was cool and collected.... He ordered his men to be deliberate and take care not to waste ammunition and not to fire unless they felt pretty sure their shots would tell. The enemy commenced firing some twenty or thirty minutes... before the Commodore suffered a gun to be fired."

Midshipman Walke reported:

"We were on the starboard tack... with the wind about east of southeast... at 6:30 tacked ship and stood for the enemy, trying to get the weather gauge of them.... The enemy hove round and stood to the southward, finding we were coming at them too fast."

Midshipman Fuller described the opening of the battle:

"At a distance of three miles their leading frigate opened fire. The shot fell short. The next one, however, passed completely over the ship.... Suddenly the *Austin* grounded and slightly heeled over to leeward.... [We saw] the Yucatan gunboats coming to our assistance, their sails white in the glistening sun, suggesting hurrying seagulls. They came down to leeward of our ships and opened on the Mexican fleet with their long 18-pounders. A freshening of the

Chapter 12

breeze together with all sail packed on the ship forced us over the shoal."

Free of the shoal, Walke reported:

"At 7:30 o'clock manned our starboard battery and exchanged five broadsides with the enemy's steamers. The [Mexican] sail vessels then on our starboard bow on the starboard tack firing on us.

"At 7:55 o'clock the enemy's sail vessels tacked to keep out of our reach when we hove in stays and fired our starboard broadside at them."

As Paixhan shells screamed overhead, Moore complained to Lt. Gray, "They won't let us get nearer. They are paddling off stern foremost faster then we can come up on them. Keep her away a little, so our broadsides can bear, and damn them, give it to them."

With excellent seamanship, the *Austin*, followed by the *Wharton*, managed to sail between the Mexican steamships and their sailing ships. They first blasted the steamers on their port beam, pouring broadsides into them.

As they came up on the enemy schooners on the downwind side to starboard, the Texans raked them with salvoes from their leeward batteries.

For some reason the highly touted British gunners were ineffective while the Texans hit home repeatedly. But like many sea battles of that age, most shots missed their targets.

Walke continued:

"At 8:10 o'clock manned the starboard battery and exchanged broadsides with the enemy's steamers, their shot passing over us. At 8:20 o'clock the steamers hove and stood to the southward to join their sail vessels...finding our shot did not reach, ceased firing."

As the two fleets maneuvered out of range, Moore piped his men to breakfast and approved a round of grog for all hands. When the Yucatan squadron passed near the two Texas ships, Captain James D. Boylan, formerly the hard-fighting skipper of the first Texas navy's warship *Brutus*, waved a greeting to his old comrades, and both flotillas loudly cheered each other.

Walke reported that by 9:30 that morning, there was "nearly a dead calm," leaving the Texans unable to press the attack.

This, of course, was the great disadvantage of sailing craft in a sea battle with steamships. The steam driven ships could, in reasonable seas, make maximum speed in all directions while sailing ships could at best maneuver no closer than 45 to 50 degrees to the wind direction.

Steamers could quickly change direction with a turn of the ship's wheel and attack or retreat at will. A direction change on a schooner or brig required a maximum crew effort to slowly bring the sails through the wind and bring the ship to a new course. Worse, with a stiff breeze and a sloppy sea, the leeward gun ports, if left open, might ship water. In any event the batteries on the leeward side would be unable to fire.

During a dead calm the sailing ships were helpless to pursue or retreat. With the wind up and when steamers held the weather gauge, sailing ships could do little but retreat.

During midmorning of the battle, with both fleets now offshore of Campeche, the Texas warships rocked almost dead in the water. It was a welcome relief to the exhausted Texas sailors, who lazed in the tropical sun waiting for the Mexican fleet to attack. They did not have to wait long. Walke recorded:

"At 11:15 o'clock the two steamers approaching us, we beat to quarters. The Yucatan vessels commenced firing on the enemy; the enemy fired several shots at them and us.

Chapter 12

Filled away on the starboard tack and exchanged several broadsides with the steamers. At 11:25 a 68-pound shot from the *Guadalupe* had cut the starboard after mizzen shroud about eight feet above the dead eye, Commodore Moore holding the shroud at the time.

"The shot passed between Commodore Moore's and Lieut. Gray's heads and would have killed both of them but that they inclined their bodies in opposite directions. The shot passed through the poop deck into the captain's cabin and out the stern about two feet above the transom.

"Up to 11:40 continued firing at the enemy, but finding that our shot did not reach them, and they having the weather gage, we kept off for Campeche. The men being completely exhausted, having been at quarters working ship with scarcely any cessation for nearly 24 hours, but in high spirits. At 11:45 Captain Boylan sent a pilot on board."

Shortly after noon, while attempting to cross the bar, the *Austin* went aground. Stuck on the bar like a stranded whale, the guns were not able to bear. Helpless, Moore feared an attack by the Mexican steamers. The light draft Yucatan boats hovered about the Texan flagship to offer some protection, but the Mexican ships had had enough fighting for one day and failed to attack.

At 12:20 the *Wharton* passed under the lee of the *Austin* steering for Campeche. Captain Lothrop hailed the grounded vessel asking if he should stand by. Moore, however, ordered him to proceed to Campeche. At 12:40 an incoming tide floated the *Austin* off the bar, and she headed toward the Campeche anchorage.

Walke wrote:

"At 1:00 p.m. one of the Mexican steamers fired several parting shots at us, which we returned, but as our shot did not reach them we ceased firing. Then the enemy vessels hauled off and stood to the south and west, we running in and anchoring off Campeche."

While many have considered the battle indecisive, arguably the advantage went to the Texans. Although the *Austin* had been hit by a big 68-pounder Paixhan missile, it had caused little damage and injured no one. The *Wharton* was hit harder when a 68-pound shot ripped into her starboard side, killing two seamen and wounding four. Neither of the Texas ships was incapacitated. Yucatan losses were not recorded.

The Texans, however, had hit the Mexican ships hard when their commanders had been rash enough to let them get within range. The *Montezuma* had fourteen men killed and thirty wounded, and the *Guadalupe* had eight killed and a score wounded.

The powerful steamers' ineffectiveness in battle sent a shock through the Mexican government, and their fleet commander, Don Francisco de Paula Lopez, was relieved of command, arrested, and court-martialed.

Commodore Lopez had been the supervising officer for the two brigs built for the Mexican navy in Baltimore shipyards in 1836. As such, he had traded shoptalk with many American naval officers and was not unfamiliar with their fighting tactics. Some said he was jinxed because both of the Baltimore ships were captured by the French during the Pastry War.

Before the revolution of 1824, when Mexico won its independence, he was a Spanish naval officer. The *New Orleans Tropic* newspaper reported that by the time of the battle, "He was an old man...deficient in energy, decision or ambition."

There were, perhaps, some extenuating circumstances for the steamers' reluctance to fight. The British captain of the *Montezuma*, Richard Cleveland, died of yellow fever the

Chapter 12

night before the battle (although Commissioner Morgan later claimed he was killed during the fighting), and fifty other British seamen were slung in their hammocks, burning up with fever.

The *Guadalupe* was also under the command of a new captain as her British skipper had resigned and returned to England shortly before the battle.

There are several other explanations for the Mexican flotilla's reluctance to close and slug it out when they could have overwhelmed the Texans with their massive firepower. With a mixed crew of English and Spanish speaking seamen who had never before fought together, the possibilities of confusion and indecision were many.

Also, while one would not question the courage of the British officers and seamen aboard the Mexican ships, one could suggest that as mercenaries they were not as willing to risk their lives as the Texans. They were apt to draw back from a slugging match that would cost them many casualties.

Although not all the men in the Texas ships were citizens of that republic, most of the officers and many of the men were dedicated to its cause. Aside from those jailbirds pressed in New Orleans, considering the lack of pay and the miseries of life at sea, there was no reason except patriotism for men to volunteer for Moore's forlorn flotilla.

Strategically, Moore had broken the blockade of Campeche by positioning himself between the Mexican fleet and their forces besieging the city, stripping the army commander of his seaborne supply route.

After the engagement, Commissioner Morgan wrote to the Texas secretary of the navy: "We have driven their fleet from Lerma and raised the blockade of Campeche. We have placed General Pedro de Ampudia, commanding the siege and his army in a very perilous situation inasmuch as he cannot now communicate with his fleet."

In a separate letter to Texas supporters, Morgan wrote:

"Their 68-pound shot was an unpleasant messenger and I never want any more of them near my head again. They are ugly customers. I beg leave to assure you their music, to me is by no means agreeable."

Commenting on the world's first naval battle in which sail fought steam, Morgan continued:

"Here we see the advantage of steam over wind and calms. It enabled the enemy to choose his distance and keep it and after fairly whipped to clear himself and save his fleet ...and now keep in full view and laugh at us. We can do nothing with their steamers except by stratagem and the moon will prevent that at this time by night while calm and light winds will place it out of our power by day.

"I could not imagine more coolness and determination than was displayed by the officers and crew in the fight... all appeared delighted and the young middies and powder boys made a perfect Jubilee of the affair. For my own part I had much rather been at a feast, for damn me if I saw any fun in it. I summoned up courage enough to keep on the deck during the action to be sure and like a frightened child who will make a noise to keep fear away, I huzzahed for Texas most of the time as loud as I could howl; but I could not help bowing instinctively to the enemy's 68-pound shot as they came over my head."

It was a letter that did much to gain public support for the sailors, who often were treated as orphans by their government and as criminals by their president. In that regard, in a letter to a friend, Morgan wrote, "I expect Old Sam will hang me—for I have traveled out of the course his instructions dictated."

Chapter 12

After returning to Campeche Bay, Moore anchored his two ships three miles from the mole because of the dangerous shoals in the area. Then he sent ashore the four men wounded on the *Wharton* to be treated at a local hospital.

While his crews enjoyed a rest and a double ration of grog, Moore, Morgan, and a few officers were rowed ashore to a tumultuous welcome by the citizens of Campeche.

For days they had been besieged by an army of from five to eight thousand men and bombarded by both land artillery and the big guns of the Mexican fleet. When told that Texas had abandoned the Yucatan cause, many had lost hope of gaining their independence. The city's officials were about to surrender when they heard the guns of Moore's fleet. The booming of the Texan's cannons, to them, was a renewed promise of deliverance.

During the fighting the citizens crowded onto the top of the city walls to watch. When the Texans interposed their ships between the Mexican fleet and the city, they cheered themselves hoarse. After the fight was over and Moore and his men came ashore, the people of Campeche greeted the Texans as conquering heroes. They lined the streets tossing flowers in the path of the Texans as they made their way to Governor Mendez' office.

There, Mendez told Moore that he had broken off negotiations with General Ampudia. Knowing that the Texas fleet was outranged by the Mexican's big guns, Mendez had two long-range 18-pounders removed from the city ramparts and put aboard the *Austin*. He then stripped a long-range 12-pounder from the walls and had it added to the *Wharton*'s armament.

Perhaps the additional long-range gunfire of the Texans, he said, would catch up to the Mexicans if they attempted to retreat from the next battle. Midshipman Fuller rejoiced, saying, "Now, if our Mexican brothers want to play a game at long bowls we can take a hand."

During the Texan's stay in Campeche, Fuller described the beleaguered city, writing:

"The city of Campeche was built by the Spaniards in the early days of the 16th century. It is a walled town, the walls being about forty feet high with open scarp and no ditch. It was intended as a defense against the natives rather than against a civilized foe. Its battery consisted of 42-pounders, mounted en barbette.... The country about, abounded in tropical fruit.... The town has no harbor, but faces an open roadstead. The bay of Campeche I think contains more sharks of all sorts and sizes than are to be found anywhere in the watery world. [There is] an extraordinary abundance of edible fish to be found in such objectionable company. The shark, however, is universally eaten in Campeche, and the fish market makes a great display of them."

In the Mexican camp, with their navy temporarily out of action, the army's artillery took up the slack and continued the bombardment of the city. Fuller recounted:

"The Mexicans as if in a satirical mood, commenced shelling the city, which they kept up for three days and nights, with slight intermissions for refreshment in the way of sleep. At the expiration of the land breeze both sides laid down their arms and gave themselves up to the inevitable siesta. When the sea breeze came in they resumed the game of war.

"Walker, Clements and I passed a cheerful hour on the ramparts working a 42-pounder. When we tired of this sport we descended and were collared by three 'grave and reverend senores,' who compelled us to sit down at a table under the shadow of the wall and regaled us with wine.

"One shot [of the Mexican artillery] should have been heard around the world when a cannon ball was sent

Chapter 12

completely through the bell in one of the cathedrals, making a perfectly round hole without cracking or shattering the bell.

"... Campeche was battered from the bombs... of the population of 70,000 all but 20,000 to 25,000 had fled." Within a few days, however, the Mexican army, probably low on ammunition, ceased firing and a welcome calm descended over the city.

After the Campeche guns were loaded aboard his ships, Moore waited for a favorable wind to enable his flotilla to sweep out of the bay and strike the Mexican fleet, still lurking out of gunshot.

Walke reported:

"May 1 to May 6 we made efforts to engage the enemy. ... They ran off to try to get us in a calm between the dying away of the land breeze and the setting in of the sea breezes ... but we were unable to get the weather gauge."

Meanwhile, the newly appointed Mexican fleet commander, Don Tomas Marin, was reinforced by the steamer *Regenerador* and two brigs of war.

On the morning of May 7, Moore's flotilla took advantage of favorable winds and sailed out, attempting to get within gun range of the Mexicans. But the breeze died and the enemy fleet skulked away. In ensuing days Moore made other attempts but could not bring the enemy fleet to battle.

In a welcome turnabout, Commodore Marin decided to do battle and on May 16 sent a challenge to Moore, daring him to come out and fight. His army allies posted a proclamation boasting:

"Those miserable adventurers who call themselves auxiliaries of Yucatan, and who suck from her miserable population $8,000 a month, will take good care not to accept the glorious challenge... because, should they be so foolhardy, the Eagle of the Aztecs...would bury in the waves these intrusive Yankees."

While Marin blustered, Moore fulminated in a letter to a friend, stating, "If I had a steamer here, I would give ten years of my life, as with it I could get to close action at once and decide the Fate of Texas."

The commodore, however, never received Marin's challenge because, during the early hours of May 16, a brisk land breeze picked up enough strength to enable the eager Texans to sail out of the bay and challenge the Mexican fleet.

Chapter 13

The Decisive Battle

In the early morning darkness of May 16, the people of Campeche began to gather on the city walls. Rumor had it that this was the day the Texans would attack the larger and more powerful squadron waiting for them offshore.

As the *Austin*, *Wharton*, and the small Yucatan ships slipped out of the bay, looking ghostly in the dim light, thousands of white handkerchiefs fluttered from the battlements in tribute to the brave men going, outnumbered and outgunned, into a fierce battle.

As dawn broke, the *Montezuma*, *Guadalupe*, two armed brigs, and two schooners were hove to a few miles off from Campeche Bay. As the Texans approached, the Mexican flotilla began standing out to sea.

Aboard the *Austin*, Midshipman Walke's minute-by-minute account of the battle, Midshipman Fuller's later description, and Commodore Moore's report give vivid accounts of the fighting. Historians would note that this was the first major battle between ships of sail matched against modern steam-driven vessels.

Walke's log:

"6:20—Beat to quarters. Cleared ship for action. Enemy's squadron under weigh, bearing southwest, distance five miles.

"6:45—Enemy standing off. Beat retreat and piped to breakfast.

"8:00—Hoisted the Texas ensign at the peak."

From his hotel room in Campeche, Commissioner Morgan later recounted that he could see "the Mexican steamers and the schooner *Aguila*. The steamers were under way under a press of steam, running out to sea. Commodore Moore and his squadron were in pursuit of them, and they kept up a running fight of several hours, until they were not visible from shore."

Moore had closed the distance to within three miles when, at about 10 o'clock, the wind died and the Texans' pursuit slowed to a turtle's pace.

Walke logged:

"10:40—*Guadalupe* hoisted English ensign, *Montezuma* the English and Spanish, and stood toward us.

"10:55—Ship headed on starboard tack, *Wharton* about half mile astern. Yucatan squadron close in shore, enemy about two and a half miles off our larboard bow commenced firing at us, most of their shot falling short."

As the Mexicans shortened the range between the flotillas, the projectiles from their big 68-pounders, which outranged the Texan guns, began to rip through the *Austin's* rigging, riddling their sails. At 11 o'clock, when the Mexican ships had closed to a scant two miles, Moore gave the order to open fire.

Walke recounted:

"11:05—Fired larboard broadside. Medium twenty-fours not reaching, ceased firing with exception of long eighteens. *Wharton* commenced firing at same time."

Chapter 13

Fuller, also aboard the *Austin*, recounts:

"At one time during this fight the commodore got a chance to square the yards, run between the two frigates, and engage them with both batteries. At the very first fire the flag staff of the *Montezuma* was shot in two, and down went the flag into the sea. That ship paddled ahead and got round on the same line with her consort, to leeward of the Texas vessels."

During a brief lull in the fighting, Moore realized the Yucatan gunboats were lagging more than three miles behind the battle. Impatiently, he hoisted flag signals ordering them to close on the enemy fleet. Although he sent numerous signals throughout the morning, for some unknown reason Boylan and his flotilla never joined in the fighting.

Fuller reported:

"The wind died out (shortly after 11 o'clock) and a short calm intervened before the sea breeze came in. The Mexicans were to leeward, but would be to windward with the coming sea breeze. The *Austin*'s yards had been braced around to meet the coming breeze, and at the very first breath of it she darted forward.

"Lothrop had not taken precaution against this, and the *Wharton* was taken aback. Her position was always on our weather quarter, but she lost so much in wearing that she fell hopelessly astern, and could not regain her position.

"I do not remember how long the combat lasted. I only know that we chased the enemy about fifteen miles. The two steamers obstinately held their position to windward, forward of our beam. It was some time before they got the range, the shots for a long while passing too high. Their guns were 68-pounders. This was the first time guns of so large a caliber were used in action."

Walke's log:

"11:18—The second shot from our long gun cut away the *Guadalupe*'s flagstaff, which fell overboard with the ensign. Crews of both vessels gave three hearty cheers.

"11:35—A thirty-two pound shot from the schooner *Aguila* passed through the larboard hammock nettings, struck coverings of steerage hatch, rebounded, struck the deck and passed out No. 7 port, wounding three men. Closing upon enemy—commenced firing medium guns."

Fuller:

"In this first shot that struck the ship, the ball taking a semicircular course, took a bite out of a sailor's heel."

Walke:

"11:40—A shot from the *Guadalupe* cut away starboard main top-gallant, breast backstay, after shroud, main top gallant rigging, starboard main royal lift and halyards, and passed through main top gallant sail.

"11:43—Shot from the *Guadalupe* cut starboard and fore top gallant steering sail yard in two.

"12:20—Sea breeze setting in but very light, the *Montezuma* being on the larboard bow, the *Guadalupe* on our larboard quarter. Put the helm up, squared the yards, manned both batteries, and ran directly between them, trying to bring them to close quarters, giving them our broadsides. As the guns bore upon them the schooner *Aguila* tacked, made all sail, and stood to the southward, and did not come into action again. The steamers, finding we were bringing them to close quarters and the wind being light, paddled off and took their position on our starboard bow."

Both the *Montezuma* and the *Guadalupe* were hit hard when the *Austin* barged between them, firing both broadsides and blasting into the steamers at close range. The decks of both Mexican warships were littered with broken

Chapter 13

bodies and dying men. One of the *Guadalupe*'s side wheels was out of action, and the entire ship was half obscured by a cloud of steam. As she limped off, she was still firing with improving accuracy and hit the *Austin* nine times with her big 68-pounder shells.

Although the *Montezuma* was also hit hard, her 68-pounder batteries also raked the *Austin* with explosive shells.

Walke:

"12:50—A 68-pound shot from the *Guadalupe* came through starboard hammock nettings over No. 7 gun, passed out larboard side carrying away forward port stanchion, No. 9 port and mizzen channels forward of the port, with two chain plates.

"1:42—The firing continuing on both sides, enemy's shot passing between our masts and over our poop. A 68-pound shot from the *Guadalupe* cut away the fourth shroud of the starboard main rigging, starboard main trap, and a foot rope of the main topsail.

"2:00—A shell exploded overhead, cutting main royal mast and several ropes starboard side, passed through the waterway and deck into the wardroom through No. 3 stateroom, purser's storeroom. It lodged in armory, wounding two men at No. 9 gun. Thomas Norris, one of the men, returned to his quarters as soon as his wounds were dressed, and in a few minutes his left arm was shot off.

"2:24—Shot from the *Guadalupe* passed through the ensign at the peak.

"2:25—A 68-pound shot from the *Guadalupe* struck the edge of the copper under No. 1 gun, breaking the plank and rebounding, causing a bad leak which was immediately plugged up.

"2:26—A shot from the *Guadalupe* cut away the third shroud of the starboard rigging and large futtock shroud.

"2:32—A 68-pound shot from *Guadalupe* passed through the hammock nettings over No. 7 gun, killing one man and wounding Midshipman A.J. Bryant, Lieut. Hubbard, gun captain Cluk and four men. One of those wounded was Cabin Steward William Barrington, one of the convicted mutineers who was sentenced to receive 100 lashes but got only fifty.

"2:35—A 68-pound shot from the *Guadalupe* struck No. 5 port starboard side, passed through and carried away both trees, ripped up the deck, injured the main topsail sheet bitts and main mast fife rail, and stopped on deck. It killed the captain of No. 5 gun and wounded two men."

Fuller:

"The missile that dismounted gun No. 5, hit Andrew Bryant, a little midshipman who was struck by a huge splinter. He had two large pieces of flesh carried away from one of his legs on both sides of the femoral artery.

"A cartridge in its leather case mysteriously exploded and blew off the arm of the powder boy who was carrying it.

"The mutineer, Frederick Shepherd, who had received no punishment, fell to the deck dead. His breast was a mass of bruises, but the surgeon said, 'Those did not kill him.' I saw a spot of blood, which induced me to kneel down and lift his hair away from the top of his forehead. A small wooden splinter two inches long had been driven into his brain."

Walke:

"2:37—*Guadalupe* badly damaged, and having trouble with one of her paddles. A shot came through the hammock nettings, over No. 6 gun starboard side, killing one man and wounding four.

"2:40—A shot cut away starboard main top gallant backstay.

Chapter 13

"2:42—A shot cut away second shroud of starboard mizzen rigging, mizzen top gallant halyards, and larboard main brace.

"2:45—A 68-pound shot came through the starboard bulwarks abaft No. 9 gun above the pin rail, wounding two men, and passed out opposite port.

"3:00—All the weather main top gallant rigging being cut away, one gun of starboard battery disabled, bore ship to engage the enemy with the larboard battery. The *Guadalupe* ceased firing and still standing on the starboard tack, we, being to leeward and not being able to bring the enemy to close quarters, kept off for Campeche. Yucatan squadron out of gunshot to leeward."

The crisp language of the naval officer gives only a slight hint of the horrors of a battle at sea. For there are the ear-shattering blasts of the cannon and the powder blackened faces of the sweat-soaked gunners. The decks are slippery with blood, gore, scattered pieces of intestines, and torn away arms and legs mingling with smashed spars. As the ships maneuver, streams of blood run out of the leeward scuppers and drain into the sea.

But perhaps the worst sight of all were the wounds inflicted by huge wooden splinters ripped from decks, masts, or spars of wooden ships. Striking a seaman by the dozen, they turned human bodies into grotesque pincushions as long shafts of torn wood penetrated halfway through a body.

During all these horrors, Midshipman Fuller recounted his own adventures:

"A curious experience is that which comes by being shot at from a long distance. One sees the flash of the gun, then hears the whistling of the ball, and then the report, the ball out-traveling the sound. After a little study of the coming balls one could determine very nearly where they were going to strike.

"Two of them I shall always remember. Of the first one I said, 'This is going to pick a man from my gun's crew.' It struck just under the port between wind and water. As it was jammed between two of the timbers it was found impossible to drive home a shot plug.

"The other shot which announced its intention to become intimate struck the deck of the topgallant forecastle directly over my head. I was at gun No. 1, and tip-tip-tipped overboard, simply denting the planks. Walker, who was master's mate of the forecastle, looked over, and with his peculiar lisp, exclaimed, 'Fuller, that was devilish close.'

"A few moments later I heard an oath from the sail maker, who declared that the scoundrels had ruined his new jib. It was of light woven duck. A cannon ball had passed through it, and the wind, freshening, was reducing it to ribbons.

"Now, some of the standing rigging having been shot away, together with a good deal of the running rigging, the commodore wore ship to take the strain off the starboard rigging and to engage the enemy with the larboard batteries.

"This heeled the starboard over to such an extent that she made water rapidly through that shot hole under gun No. 1, and absolutely compelled a return to our anchorage."

Hit seventeen times, with most of her starboard rigging in tatters, the *Austin* was in danger of losing one or more of her masts. Moore later reported that going about on a port tack to ease the pressure on the weakened starboard rigging, the ship heeled over. This put the shot hole along the starboard waterline under water, causing the *Austin*'s magazine to become flooded with more than three feet of water.

Chapter 13

Cursing, Moore had to call off the chase, and signaling the *Wharton* to follow, he limped back to Campeche Bay.

During the course of the battle, the Texans had chased the Mexican fleet more than fifteen miles, driving them back toward their base at Telchac.

After the *Austin* dropped anchor in Campeche Bay, Moore had his wounded transferred to a local hospital. Then, in a fury, he sent for Captain Boylan, commander of the Yucatan squadron, which had hung back from the fight. When Boylan came aboard the *Austin*, Moore lashed out at him, charging him with cowardly behavior.

Not engaging in a fight was strange behavior from Boylan, for while he skippered the *Brutus* he was always eager to engage an enemy, regardless of the odds. His response to the charges is not known, but one is inclined to consider that the reluctance to fight came from the Yucatan officers. They were probably reluctant to pit their small ships against the Mexican steamers' 68-pounder guns when one well-placed shot could cripple or sink any ship in their flotilla.

In assessing the results of the battle, Fuller reported:

"The *Montezuma* was so crippled that it was twenty minutes before she could stir. The *Guadalupe* followed after us for a short distance and then returned back to her consort. The sailing vessels of the Mexican fleet fled at the moment the sea breeze came in.

"The most unaccountable mystery connected with this fight is that a superior force, more than three to one, fled from their adversaries."

The *Austin*, which had been hit repeatedly by the huge 68-pounder shells, suffered three dead: seamen Frederick Shepherd, William West, and George Baryon. There were a number of crippling wounds suffered by others. Seaman Owen Timothy had his left leg amputated, Thomas Barnett had his arm torn off at the elbow, Thomas Norris had his left arm ripped off at the shoulder. Midshipman Bryant, only fourteen years old, had part of his right hand shot off and suffered a serious wound on his right leg. Marine Private George Davis had part of his right foot shot off, and sixteen others were wounded, some seriously. On board the *Wharton*, two gunners were killed when the barrel of an 18-pounder, loaded improperly, exploded.

Several days after the battle, an English sailor, deserting from their navy, reported the Mexican losses. He stated that the *Guadalupe* had 47 men killed, 32 had limbs amputated, and 64 others were severely wounded. The *Montezuma*, he said, had 40 killed and more than 20 seriously wounded.

Both sides, of course, claimed victory. The Mexican commander, Commodore Marin, without mentioning his heavy casualties, reported that by late afternoon the Texans had retreated to Campeche Bay. He did not mention that the Texans had chased him for fifteen miles, trying to close with him so that their short-range guns could come into play.

Marin fatuously claimed victory, stating the Texans were bottled up at Campeche; but he avoided reporting that whenever Moore came out, he retreated.

Some historians have written that the two battles were inconclusive, and tactically this might be considered true. But strategically, Moore's expedition into Mexican waters was a decisive victory for Texas.

Similarly, but on a much more massive scale, one can recall the World War I naval battle at Jutland in 1916 between the British and German fleets. While the German High Seas Fleet gained a minor tactical victory in the battle, it was a decisive strategic defeat for them. Never again would they challenge the British, who maintained their control of the sea lanes for the remainder of the war.

Chapter 13

The two battles off the Yucatan coast left the Texas navy dominant in the Gulf of Mexico. The Mexican navy had no stomach for another battle with Moore's flotilla. This became even more evident when, on June 14, the enlistments of the British mercenaries serving on the three Mexican steamships expired. They too had no desire to risk their lives against a Texas navy hell-bent on closing with them for a fight to the finish.

In any event, with the departure of the British, the Mexicans had neither the trained mechanics to keep the steamships operable nor the experienced gunners to man their formidable Paixhan gun batteries.

Moore's domination of the Mexican waters enabled the Yucatan government to obtain more favorable conditions for remaining in the Mexican union.

Never again would the Mexican navy attempt to blockade the Texas coast and strangle the commerce of the young republic. As Commissioner Morgan wrote, "We knocked hell into them.... We thrashed them soundly and the whole fleet ran off."

Of the greatest importance to Texas, however, was that any ambitions of Santa Anna to launch a seaborne invasion of the new republic were finally shattered for all time. Texas, in fact, was finally free from the threat of further invasions from Mexico. Texans were able to live and flourish in peace until December 1845 when they became the twenty-eighth state of the United States of America.

Chapter 14

Valor Betrayed

While repairing damage to the *Austin* in Campeche Bay, Moore arranged with the Yucatan authorities to have Lieutenant A.G. Gray take command of their schooner *Independencia* for a raid on Telchac. The small northern Yucatan port was being used as a base for Mexican navy ships and as a supply depot for the Mexican army. In late May Gray and a crew of Texans completed the 150-mile sail to Telchac, where they harried Mexican commerce and captured a supply ship named *Glide*.

To take on fresh water and gain intelligence on Mexican movements, Gray put into the friendly port of Sisal. There he heard from an American ship captain that Houston had published his proclamation labeling Moore and his officers as pirates.

When Moore and Commissioner Morgan finally received a copy of the missive on May 30, they were shocked to read:

"I, Sam Houston, President, and Commander-in-Chief of the Army and Navy of the Republic of Texas, do, by these presents, declare and proclaim, that he, the aforesaid Post

Chapter 14

Captain, E.W. Moore is suspended from all command in the Navy of the Republic....

"And I do further declare and proclaim, on failure of obedience to this command... that this Government will no longer hold itself responsible for his acts upon the high seas; but in such case, requests all the governments in treaty, or on terms of amity with this government, and all naval officers on the high seas or in ports foreign to this country, to seize the said Post Captain, E. W. Moore, the ship *Austin* and the brig *Wharton*, with their crews, and bring them, or any of them, into the port of Galveston, that the vessels may be secured to the Republic, and the culprit or culprits arraigned and punished by the sentence of a legal tribunal.

"The Naval Powers of Christendom will not permit such a flagrant and exampled outrage... to pass unrebuked; for such would be to destroy all civil rule and establish a precedent which would jeopardize the commerce on the ocean and render encouragement and sanction to piracy."

As a reward for saving Texas from invasion, Moore, his officers, and possibly Commissioner Morgan were liable to be attacked by any "Naval Power of Christendom" and brought in chains to Galveston to be tried as pirates. Houston apparently would not be satisfied until he could see the bodies of the heroes of the Campeche battles dangling from a gibbet.

In a letter to his friend Swartwout, Colonel Morgan summed up the results of the Campeche campaign, writing that if Houston had not prevented them:

"We would have captured all the Mexican fleet—beyond doubt by a night attack. We could not catch the steamer in the day time. But we saved Galveston which was to have been taken possession of forthwith and... General Ampudia intended landing on Galveston with 10,000 troops. He had three Steamers and five armed vessels and 20 troop vessels. If Galveston had fallen into their hands Texas was gone."

Of some relief to the dispirited men of the Texas navy was Swartwout's assurance that the people of Texas supported their efforts. He wrote:

"That document of the President's, has created a feeling of deepest horror... amongst all the friends of Houston and of Texas. Not a man of any party justifies it and most men put the worst and most discreditable construction upon the act. Houston will have trouble about the business. You and Col. Moore will be honored for ever, for the course you took.... The people of Texas will defend him and you with their lives....

"[Houston] is openly and vociferously charged here, with being a Traitor to his country and in the interest and pay of Santa Anna. This is horrible, but not more strange than his own conduct... I will never believe that Sam Houston... is capable of a corrupt act, but the Devil of it is, that he has espoused the cause of the enemy which no one can justify.... While Santa Anna is decimating Texian prisoners of war and dooming the [rest]... to the most severe and loathsome slavery, Houston is denouncing as Pirates and Robbers... his fellow citizens who are endeavoring to diminish his power of doing this mischief and these wrongs to the citizens of Texas. There is a mystery about his conduct, that he must clear up as fast as possible or he is gone."

On June 14 Moore learned of the British mercenaries' departure from Mexico. Swartwout's reassurances notwithstanding, Moore and Morgan agreed that they should make no further attacks on the now almost helpless Mexican fleet. It was necessary, they agreed, that they should return to Galveston as soon as possible.

Chapter 14

On mutual agreement Moore and Governor Mendez terminated their alliance after the Yucatan government paid for all of the repairs to the *Austin* and provided the Texas fleet with a resupply of gunpowder.

On June 25 the Mexican fleet and all of the army troops in the Campeche area retreated from their temporary base in Telchac and sailed north to Veracruz. The Mexican navy would never again fight the Texans. Moore's small flotilla was now the undisputed master of the Gulf of Mexico.

On June 29, with all repairs completed, the *Austin* and the *Wharton* sailed for home to the cheers of the people of Campeche.

Commissioner Morgan had earlier sent a defiant letter to Texas friends by way of a merchant ship heading for Galveston, in which he proclaimed:

"As the nations of Christendom will be on the lookout for us on our return, I presume we will have to run the gauntlet. There is one thing certain, we won't be taken. Our colors will be nailed to the masthead.

"In the affair of the 30th, when there was good reason to believe we would be overpowered, the match was ready for the magazine, an event not joyfully anticipated, but joyfully concurred in by every soul on board. It is not to be supposed that we will be less determined now, when we are fighting with a halter round our necks.

"Fragments of our gallant barques will be the only trophy for the nations of Christendom to exult over, and when these fragments are rescued from the billows, fragments of other ships will be seen floating by their side, for our last struggle will be a Sampson grapple."

The fleets of Christendom, however, gave a wide berth to the battle-hardened Texans. Moore ordered a final stop at his old rendezvous anchorage at the Alacranes Islands. There the crew gathered thirty-five turtles for a feast of

Valor Betrayed

The 400-ton brig *Wharton* armed with fifteen 18-pounders fought alongside the *Austin* during the victorious sea battles off Campeche. The battles marked the first time sailing vessels fought against steam-driven ships of war. (Courtesy of the Rosenberg Library, Galveston, Texas)

meat and soup. Then, unmolested, they continued their passage to Galveston.

On the morning of July 15, the two ships crossed the bar and entered Galveston Bay. As they drew up by a wharf in the harbor, the citizens of Galveston rushed to the ships cheering. Local militia units fired a twenty-one-gun salute, honoring the men and the battered ships that they believed had saved their city.

When Moore and his men came ashore, Mayor John M. Allen and other dignitaries made welcoming speeches to the "heroes who had saved Texas." When the officers and men of the flotilla marched through the city to the location where they would be wined and dined, they were escorted by companies of the local militia. To the music of the

Chapter 14

Galveston City Band, the ladies of Galveston tossed flowers in their path and draped them with gay-colored ribbons.

Commander Moore sent a message to the sheriff of Galveston County, stating he was ready to surrender and stand trial for piracy. The sheriff, however, refused to place him under arrest or take him into custody.

Houston, receiving word of the lionization of his enemies, decided it would not be expedient to have Moore and his men tried for piracy. On July 25, without a hearing or a court-martial, he signed papers dishonorably discharging Moore, Lothrop, and Lieutenant C.B. Snow from the naval service. Colonel Morgan was fired from his post as commissioner, and most of the sailors were discharged.

On July 26 Moore made his departure from the *Austin*. As he walked down the gangplank for the last time, the crew fired a thirteen-gun salute and gave three roaring cheers for the man who had led them to victory against overwhelming odds. And as Lothrup bid goodbye to his crew on the *Wharton*, they saluted him with eight guns and loud cheering.

The following day all the officers of the Texas navy, except one lieutenant and a sailing master, resigned their commissions in disgust.

Moore demanded the right to a trial, and in February 1844 a joint committee of the Congress granted his request. In their report, which sent Houston into a rage, they charged that the president had violated the law in arbitrarily dismissing Moore. They accused Houston of denying the commodore the "opportunity of defending a reputation acquired by severe trials, privations, and hardships, in sustaining the honor and glory of the flag under which he had sailed and fought."

The report further stated:

"... it was worse than cruel thus to have branded with infamy and disgrace a name heretofore bright and unsullied on the pages of our history, and to have driven from our shores, as an outcast upon the world, one whose long and well-tried services, all appreciate and approve."

On August 21, 1844, Moore was tried by court-martial on charges of misapplication of funds, embezzlement of public property, neglect of duty, disobedience to orders, contempt and defiance of law, treason, and murder. The murder indictment was a result of Houston's charge that Moore had, without authority, hung the New Orleans mutineers, thus committing an act of murder.

Undoubtedly swaying the jury's verdict was Commissioner Morgan's testimony that it was under the authority granted to him by the Texas Congress that he authorized Moore's attack on the Mexican navy in order to "save Texas."

Morgan testified:

"General Houston had assured me in the winter [of 1842], during the session of Congress, that there was to be a formidable invasion of the country; that 'It was gone and out of his power to save it [Texas], that it would cease to be a Republic in six months.'

"I was induced to hazard the responsibility of suggesting to Commodore Moore to take Telchac and the coast of Yucatan, on our way out to Galveston to save the Republic."

The court found Moore innocent of all charges, except for a count of disobedience of orders, for which they assessed no penalty.

The verdict threw Houston into another rage, and he vengefully denounced the court's verdict, charging that they had erred and that Moore was, in fact, guilty on all charges.

Chapter 14

Captain Lothrop was also cleared of all charges before a military court-martial. Sadly, three months later, in August 1844, while serving as a captain of a merchant ship, he was stricken with yellow fever and died suddenly. Lothrop was one of the oldest officers in terms of his seven years of service in both the first and second Texas navies. He was only thirty years old.

Lieutenant Snow was also tried and found not guilty of all charges.

In November 1844 the four remaining Texas ships, the *Austin*, *Wharton*, *Archer*, and the repaired *San Bernard*, were put up for sale to the highest bidder. The news spread through Galveston like a plague virus. Enraged citizens were out in the streets screaming defiance at Houston and swearing the sale would never take place. Effigies of Houston were burned in the streets.

On the day of the auction, hundreds of grim-faced men, clutching rifles and fingering their new Colt six-shooters, marched to the place of sale. As they surged toward a frightened auctioneer, waving their weapons, they screamed, "No bids. No bids."

As the auctioneer, in a weak voice, asked, "What am I offered?" An ominous silence came over the crowd. Fierce glances from angry armed men swept over the assembled people. Silence. The proud ships of the Texas navy were to remain Texan. They were, however, placed in ordinary and began to rot away from neglect.

But thanks to the battles off Campeche, they were no longer needed. The Mexican navy had been rendered impotent, and perhaps more importantly, the annexation of Texas by the United States was becoming imminent. United States Presidents John Tyler and James Polk instructed the American navy to protect Texas commerce in the Gulf. With American warships under the command of Commodore

Robert Stockton on patrol, Texas shipping, for the first time in a decade, was safe from interference by foreign powers.

In May 1845 Moore, embittered by his constant harassment, wrote a letter to Sam Houston that to a man of honor would have provoked a duel:

"Galveston, May 5, 1845,

"E.W. Moore to General Sam Houston,

"Sir, I herewith enclose a copy of a statement to the people of Texas of some of your sayings and doings in relation to myself while you were President of this Republic.

"I would willingly adopt another course, and demand of you that redress which one gentleman has a right to expect from another who has abused, vilified, and misrepresented him, as you have me on so many occasions, in public bar rooms, in the streets, and even in the presence of ladies, but for the well known fact that you have refused to render satisfaction to General Lamar, Judge Burnett, and Doctor Archer, for gross and flagrant acts of injustice which you have done them.

"There is one other resort—that of chastising you publicly—which I would adopt, were it not well known that you had submitted to be thus disgraced by Colonel Jordan, in the town of Austin, while you were a member of Congress.... My arrival here the day before yesterday as well as yours at the same time, affords me this opportunity of apprising you of my intention to show up your true character to the citizens of Texas, as well as to the world, which I will continue to do from time to time, unless you notify me that you will render me redress for the repeated acts of ungentlemanly conduct of which you have been guilty towards myself, to gratify a pitiful spirit of revenge....

"You were elected by the good ... people of Texas to the highest office within their gift, which you prostituted in so

Chapter 14

many instances to gratify your craven and vindictive propensities."

In a public statement Houston made a mocking reply:

"Now it is very well known that I had quit bar-rooms in 1845, and I only patronized them in a small way before that. 'In public bar-rooms, in the streets, and even in the presence of ladies.' That was a most inelegant thing on my part! Surely I ought never to have abused him before ladies. Why, Sir, for me to depreciate such a gallant gentleman in the presence of ladies, after his great feat of dodging cannon balls, would not be exactly clever on my part.

"Mark you, he says, he would have demanded satisfaction from me 'but for the well known fact that you have refused to render satisfaction to General Lamar, Judge Burnett, and Doctor Archer, for gross and flagrant acts of injustice.'

"I never had a correspondence with any of these gentlemen... or a quarrel with any one of the three named. To be sure, they did not like me, but that was their fault, not mine. I will avail myself of this occasion now to declare that I never made a quarrel with a mortal man on earth; nor will I ever do anything to originate a quarrel with any man, woman or child living."

Even Houston supporters must have had to suppress a chuckle at Houston's self-appraisement since he was one of the most quarrelsome and vindictive men in the history of a Texas noted for personal vendettas.

Houston, who had acquired an unearned reputation as a fighting leader, tried to make a joke out of the challenge, stating:

"I would not fight a duel. One of the gentlemen referred to did send me a verbal challenge... sent on a Saturday night, to meet the challenger the next morning. I objected to it [because] we were to meet on Sunday morning, and

Valor Betrayed

that I did not think anything was to be made by fighting on that day... also he was a good Christian, and had had his child baptized the Sunday before. [Finally] that I never fought down hill. He seemed to be satisfied with this good-humored answer, and it is the only challenge I have ever received in Texas."

Moore supporters were not amused. The commodore sent copies of his letter to Galveston newspapers, who published it in full. Houston continued to ignore the public insults.

In a published pamphlet, "Doings of the Texas Navy," Moore sneered, "General Sam Houston has refused on repeated occasions to render that redress to which gentlemen are sometimes compelled to resort."

In June 1846 Texas was annexed by the United States. By then all of the Texas ships but the *Austin* had rotted in the harbor and were rejected by the United States Navy. Later they were sold at auction for a pittance. A short time later the *Austin* was also reduced to a rotting wreck, judged not worth repairing, and broken up.

For years the feud between Houston and Moore continued. If the verbal barrages had been bullets, both of the combatants would have expired on the field of battle.

Houston exercised his apparent hatred for the Texas navy in a message to the Senate in which he denied bounty land "to the officers, seamen and marines of the navy." As he often did, he first couched his refusal in terms of praise; the venom came later. He wrote:

"I herewith return to your Honorable body without my signature a bill authorizing and requiring the Secretary of War and Navy to issue certificates of bounty land to the officers, seamen and marines of the navy.

"I do so with a full appreciation of the exalted gallantry and distinguished bravery of our naval forces from the

Chapter 14

moment that our flag was first unfurled to the breeze on the bosom of the gulf down to the present hour.

"But while I admit all this, with feelings of pride and pleasure, there are considerations which lend me to the conviction that to permit the bill to pass without the negative of the executive, would be little less than a sanction of injudicious and unnecessary extravagance...

"Bounties in lands have at different times been granted to the army, but never to the navy. Generally, the seaman has no interest, except a transitory one, on shore. His professional pursuits forbid that attention to the use and improvement of grants of this kind, which alone could result in benefit to either the recipient or the country.

"To make such grants would, in a large majority of cases, be the very perfection of prodigality. The harpies that are usually found in sea ports and to whom seamen usually become indebted are those only who would profit by the bounty and munificence of the government.

"Sailors who would have claims are either dead or scattered before the winds of Heaven. If bounty land were granted, the few who survive would deem it valueless because none of them would be willing to penetrate the wilderness in quest of a place to locate it some hundreds of miles beyond our frontiers; and rather than make the attempt they would be willing to sell it for a trifle.

"The heirs of deceased sailors would not be benefited by their claims. Persons would be found... to defraud the legal heirs, should they ever come forward to claim the promised bounty."

So much for Houston's "pride and pleasure" at the "exalted gallantry and distinguished bravery of our naval forces."

In private letters and in public harangues, Houston, while a United States Senator from Texas, continued to speak of "that miserable Commodore Moore...who would fall by his own poison or be strangled by his own venom.... He, like a bloated maggot, can only live in his own corruption."

Houston derided Moore's heroism in battle, stating that the commodore never fought for Texas but only served Yucatan. He pretended there had never been a battle with the Mexican fleet off Campeche. And he continued to claim that the Texas navy never accomplished anything of value for the new republic.

Moore responded in kind. His version of the truth was accepted by the Texas legislature and many Texans who continued to honor his service to the republic.

While his days as a Texas naval officer were over, in 1848, although Houston attempted to prevent it, the Texas Legislature awarded Moore $11,398.36. Later they voted an additional $15,202.06 in compensation for the funds he had spent out of his own pocket to purchase supplies from New Orleans shipyards. They also awarded him $3,500 in back pay. In 1856 he received another $9,000 for back pay in a final financial settlement. In later years Moore married and moved to New York. Forgotten, he died in 1865.

A joint resolution of the Texas Congress awarded half pay for life to eight of the disabled seamen and marines who fought in the Campeche battles.

The Congress also appropriated $76,000 in back pay to be distributed to the officers of the Texas navy. Those officers were rejected for commissions in the American navy after a heated dispute. But as compensation, they were awarded pay for five years equal to that of an officer of equal rank in the United States Navy.

Thus ended the troubled but glorious life of the navy of the Republic of Texas.

L'Envoi

Texans for more than a century and a half have honored the heroes of the Texas fight for independence. Bowie, Travis, Crockett, Seguin, Bonham, Lamar, and Houston have a hallowed place in the hearts of all Texans. Statues have been sculpted in their likeness, museums have honored their artifacts, and schoolchildren have been taught of their heroism.

But the courageous seamen of the Texas navy have been all but forgotten.

For more than a decade, they fought the fury of Gulf storms and braved the guns of a powerful fleet, all the while reviled as outlaws by their president. But against all odds they triumphed.

The first Texas navy dominated the Gulf of Mexico. They captured ships laden with supplies for Santa Anna's armies and turned them over to the ill-equipped troops commanded by Sam Houston.

Some military analysts believe that without the gunpowder captured from the *Pelicano* the Texas army could not have fought the battle of San Jacinto.

Texas naval ships and Texas privateers raised havoc with Mexican shipping. They prevented reinforcements from reaching Santa Anna and made impossible the imposition of an enemy blockade, which would have strangled Texas's economic lifeline with the United States.

The second navy, under Commodore Moore, ravaged the Mexican coast for three years. This enabled Yucatan forces to resist the Centralist government, thus draining off

L'Envoi

Mexican troops and ships that would have otherwise been used for a seaborne invasion of Texas.

In the first and only sea battle in which outmoded sailing ships firing cast-iron cannon balls fought modern steam-driven warships armed with improved explosive shells, the Texans won a decisive strategic victory.

Commodore Edwin Ward Moore, the commanding officer of the Texas navy, although outnumbered and outgunned, won a decisive strategic sea battle against a powerful Mexican fleet in the waters off Campeche. (Center for American History, University of Texas, Austin)

L'Envoi

Although outnumbered and outgunned, Moore's battles in the Gulf waters off Campeche saved Texas from a seaborne invasion that might have destroyed the new republic.

As an aftermath, the Texas navy's undisputed domination of the Gulf forced Mexico into a de facto armistice until Texas was annexed by the United States.

Without these fierce men of the sea, it is doubtful Texas could have either won its independence or maintained it for a perilous decade.

Naval strategy is but little known among Texas historians. Invasions that were not mounted, battles that were not fought, and an economy that was not strangled because of the decisive use of sea power are little noted.

Today the men who sailed and fought those battered ships are unknown to the people of Texas and ignored by Texas historians. They deserve better.

In the pantheons of Texas heroes, there should be writ large the names of: Captains James D. Boylan, Jeremiah and William Brown, Midshipman C.C. Cox, Secretary of the Navy Samuel Rhoads Fisher, Midshipman George F. Fuller, Captains Nathaniel Hoyt, William Hurd, Daniel L. Kokernut.

And Commander John Lothrop, Midshipman James L. Mabry, Colonel James Morgan, Captains Henry and Thomas Thompson, Midshipman Alfred Walke, Commander George Wheelwright, and many others.

And forever enshrined in the hearts of all Texans—Commodore Edwin Ward Moore.

Bibliography

Archival Material

Texas State Archives, Texas State Library, Austin:

"A Brief Synopsis of the Doings of the Texas Navy, Under Command of Commodore E.W. Moore" by E.W. Moore.

"To the People of Texas" by E.W. Moore

"Reply to the Pamphlet by Commanders Buchanan, Dupont, and Magruder of the United States Navy."

E.W Moore, Miscellaneous File.

Navy Papers.

Midshipman's Journal and Log Book of Alfred Walke, Texas Navy.

Diplomatic Correspondence of the Republic of Texas. Vol. II. Part I; Part III.

Center of American History, University of Texas, Austin:

Logbook of Midshipman Edward Johns, Texas Navy.

Lieutenant Tennison's Journal. Texas Navy.

James Mabry Journal. Texas Navy.

Captain James D. Boylan, Commander of Schooner of War *Brutus* to Honorable Secretary of the Navy, August 31, 1837.

"Report of the Cruise and Transactions of the Texian schooner of war *Brutus*."

Boylan to Secretary of the Navy. September 1, 1837.

Bibliography

Henry L. Thompson, commanding Texas Navy to the Honorable Naval Department August 29, 1837. "Report Relative to My Cruise in Command of the Texas Fleet."

William M. Shepherd, Secretary of the Texas Navy to R.A. Irion, Secretary of State of the Republic of Texas. May 1, 1838.

Shepherd to President of the Republic. Sept 30, 1837.

Irion to Shepherd, April 26, 1838.

Francis B. Wright to Secretary of the Texas Navy. September 20, 1837.

E.W. Moore to Secretary of War and Navy. August 28, 1840.

Moore to Secretary of War George Washington Hockley. February 6, 1842.

Moore to Hockley. April 5, 1842.

Rosenberg Library, Galveston:

James Morgan Papers:

James Morgan to James Reed. May 11, 1843.

Samuel Swartwout to Morgan. June 1, 1843.

Morgan to Swartwout. August 1, 1843.

Swartwout to Morgan. September 1, 1843.

Books

Bass, Feris A. & Brunson, B.R. (ed.) *Fragile Empires: The Texas Correspondence of Samuel Swartwout & James Morgan 1836-1856*. Shoal Creek Publishers: Austin. 1978.

Bauer, K. Jack & Roberts, Stephen S. *Register of Ships of the United States Navy 1775-1990*. Greenwood Press: N.Y. 1991.

Bollaert, William. *William Bollaert's Texas*. University of Oklahoma Press: Norman. 1956.

Canney, Donald L. *United States Coast Guard & Revenue Cutters*. Naval Institute Press: Annapolis. 1995.

Cartwright, Gary. *Galveston: A History of the Island*. Atheneum: N.Y. 1991.

Chapelle, Howard I. *The History of the American Sailing Navy*. W.W. Norton & Co.: N.Y. 1949.

Cochran, Hamilton. *Noted American Duels and Hostile Encounters*. Chilton Books: N.Y. 1963.

Devereaux, Linda Ericson. *The Texas Navy*. Ericson Books: Nacogdoches, Texas. 1983.

Douglas, Claude L. *Thunder on the Gulf*. Turner Company. 1936.

DeBruhl, Marshal. *Sword of San Jacinto: A Life of Sam Houston*. Random House: N.Y. 1993.

Fehrenbach, T.R. *Lone Star: A History of Texas and the Texans*. American Legacy Press: N.Y. 1983 edition.

Foote, Henry S. *Texas and the Texans*. The Steck Company: Austin. 1935.

Francaviglia, Richard V. *From Sail to Steam: Four Centuries of Texas Maritime History 1500-1900*. University of Texas Press: Austin. 1998.

Gambrell, Herbert. *Anson Jones, The Last President of Texas*. Doubleday & Co.: Garden City. 1948.

_____. *Mirabeau Buonaparte Lamar, Troubadour and Crusader*. Southwest Press: Dallas. 1934.

Gracy, Davis B. & Carefoot, Jean. *Ships of the Texas Navy*. Presidial Press: Austin. 1978.

Henson, Margaret Swett. *Juan Davis Bradburn, A Reappraisal of the Mexican Commander at Anahuac*. Texas A&M Press: College Station. 1982.

Hill, Jim Dan. *The Texas Navy, in Forgotten Battles and Shirtsleeve Diplomacy*. University of Chicago Press. 1937.

James, Marquis. *The Raven: A Biography of Sam Houston*. Halcyon House: Garden City. 1949.

Kane, Harnet C. *Gentlemen, Swords and Pistols*. William Morrow & Co.: N.Y. 1951.

Bibliography

Krauze, Enrique. *Mexico: Biography of a People*. Harpers Collins: New York. 1997.

Long, Jeff. *Duel of Eagles*. William Morrow & Co., N.Y. 1990.

McDonald, Archie P. *Travis*. The Pemberton Press: Austin. 1976.

Meyer, Michael C. & William L. Sherman. *The Course of Mexican History*. Oxford University Press: N.Y. 1987.

Moore, Commodore Edwin W. *To the People of Texas, In Vindication of his Conduct of the Navy, 1843*. Center for American History, The University of Texas: Austin.

Nance, Joseph M. *Attack and Counterattack*. University of Texas Press: Austin. 1964.

Robinson, Admiral Samuel Murray, USN, retired. *A Brief History of the Texas Navies*. Sons of the Republic of Texas: Houston. 1961.

Ruiz, Ramon Eduardo. *Triumph & Tragedy, A History of the Mexican People*. W.W. Norton & Co.: N.Y. 1992.

Thrall, Rev. Homer S. *A Pictorial History of Texas*. N.D. Thompson & Co.: St. Louis, Missouri. 1879.

Turner, Martha Anne. *Travis - His Sword and His Pen*. Texian Press: Waco. 1972.

Wells, Commander Tom Henderson, USN, retired. *Commodore Moore and the Texas Navy*. University of Texas Press: Austin. 1960.

Werner, Michael S. *Encyclopedia of Mexico*. Fitzroy Dearborn Publishers: Chicago. 1997.

Williams, Amelia W. & Barker, Eugene C. (ed.) *The Writings of Sam Houston*. Volumes 1-8. The University of Texas Press: Austin. 1938-1943.

Winkler, E.W. (ed.) *Secret Journals of the Senate, Republic of Texas 1836-1845*. Austin Printing Company: Austin. 1911.

Magazines and Scholarly Journals

Adams, Ephriam Douglass (ed.) "British Correspondence Concerning Texas." *Texas Historical Quarterly.* Vol. 15. 1911.

Barker, Eugene C. "The African Slave Trade in Texas." *Texas Historical Association Quarterly.* Vol. 6. 1902.

"Difficulties of a Mexican Revenue Officer in Texas." *Texas Historical Association Quarterly.* Vol. 4. No. 3. January 1901.

Carter, Robert Foster. "The Texan Navy." *U.S. Naval Institute Proceedings 59, No. 365.* 1935.

Cox, C.C. "Reminiscences of C.C. Cox." *Texas Historical Association Quarterly.* Vol. 6. 1902.

Daniel, James M. "The Ships of the Texas Navy and Ships Acting With the Government of Texas." *Southwestern Historical Quarterly.* 1947.

Dienst, Dr. Alexander. "The Navy of the Republic of Texas" *Quarterly of the Texas State Historical Association.* Part I. Vol. 12. 1908-January 1909.

Part II. Vol. 12. April 1909.

Part III. Vol. 13. July 1909.

Part IV. Vol. 13. October 1909.

Fuller, George F. "Sketch of the Texas Navy." *Southwestern Historical Quarterly.* Vol. VII. January 1904.

Harris, George F. "History of the Texas Navy." *Southwestern Historical Quarterly.* Vol. LXIII. April 1960.

Haugh, George F. (ed.) "History of the Texas Navy." *Southwestern Historical Quarterly.* Vol. LXIII. April 1960.

"The Texas Navy at New York." *Southwestern Historical Quarterly.* Vol. LXIV. January 1961.

Kokernot, D.L. "Battle of Anahuac." *Southwestern Historical Quarterly.* Vol. XLII. 1939.

Looscan, Adele B. "The Old Fort at Anahuac." *Texas Historical Association Quarterly.* Vol. 1. July 1898.

Bibliography

Moore, Major General Marc A. USMC, retired. "Marines of the Texas Republic." *Marine Corps Gazette*. August 1978.

Nance, Joseph M. "Woll's Report 1842." *Southwestern Historical Quarterly*. Vol. LVIII. 1954-1955.

Neu, C.T. "The Case of the Brig Pocket." *Texas Historical Association Quarterly*. Vol. 12. April 1909.

Wells, Tom H. "An Evaluation of the Texas Navy." *Southwestern Historical Quarterly*. Vol. LXIII. 1960.

Worley, J.L. "Diplomatic Relations of England and the Republic of Texas." *Texas Historical Association Quarterly*. Vol. IX. July 1905.

Newspapers

Galveston Civilian. 5-31-1843.

Galveston News. 12-10-1844; 1-9, 1-16, 2-13-1893 (James Mabry Journal); 10-8-1899; 5-23-1902; 3-1-1903.

Houston Morning Star. 7-25-1843.

New Orleans Courier. 1-16-1836.

New Orleans Picayune. 12-20-1844.

Telegraph & Texas Register. 10-15-1837; 2-22, 3-2, 3-18- 1842; 10-18-1843.

Texas Gazette. 1-30, 4-17-1830.

Texas Republican. 9-19-1835.

Glossary of Nautical Terms

Aback—A sail blown back by the wind against the direction of the ship's travel, thus slowing the forward movement of the ship.

Abeam—A wide angle to the center line of the ship.

Astern—To the rear of the ship.

Bar—A ridge or partially submerged bank, usually of sand, which obstructs entrance to a harbor.

Barrier islands—Islands parallel to the shore and separated from it by a lagoon.

Beat to quarters—A summons to the crew, usually by drum, to take battle positions.

Beating against the wind—To sail the ship at an angle toward the direction from which the wind blows.

Boatswain—A naval petty officer.

Bone in her teeth—Sailing fast with white water breaking across the bow.

Boom—A wooden spar to which a sail is attached.

Bow chaser—A long-range cannon placed at the front of the ship.

Bowsprit—A spar projecting from the front of the ship to which a corner of the jib sail is attached.

Breakers—White water caused by bars or shoals.

Brig—A two-masted, square rigged ship.

Carronade—A short barreled, short-range cannon.

Close-hauled—Sailing as close as possible to the direction of the wind.

Glossary of Nautical Terms

Cutter—A fore and aft rigged ship with one mast, a mainsail and several jib sails.

Deadeye—A block through which ship's lines are passed.

Displacement—The weight of water displaced by a ship when afloat.

Draft—The depth of water needed to float a ship.

Fathom—Six feet.

Fore and aft rig—Sails rigged on masts in a line from front to back. This rig, used on schooners and other vessels, is highly maneuverable in coastal waters.

Foretopman—A sailor whose duties require him to work on sails at or near the top of the ship's masts.

Gaffsail—A gaff is a spar hoisted at the rear side of a mast to support the top of a quadrilateral sail.

Gig—A light ship's boat propelled by oars.

Go about—To change direction through the wind so as to bring it to the other side of the sails.

Grog—Rum diluted with water.

Heave to—To trim the sails and rudder so that the ship lies stationary in the water.

Helm alee—A command given when moving the bow through the eye of the wind.

Jib sails—Triangular sails set forward of the mast.

Jolly Roger—Pirate flag. Usually a white skull and crossbones on a black background.

Jury rig—An improvised rig erected when masts, lines, or sails have been blown away or damaged.

Knot—A unit of speed and time. One knot equals one nautical mile per hour. A common redundancy is to use "knots per hour."

Land breeze—A breeze blowing from land to sea.

Leadsman—A sailor who uses a pole or sounding lead to determine the depth of water.

Glossary of Nautical Terms

Letter of Marque—A license given by a government to a ship owner to fit out an armed ship to attack and capture enemy ships.

Longboat—A small boat carried on a ship, which is propelled by oars.

Lubber—A person ignorant of seamanship.

Luff—To bring the ship's bow directly into the wind.

Mizzenmast—The shorter mast aft of the mainmast.

Offshore wind—A wind moving from the shore toward the sea.

Onshore wind—A wind moving from the sea toward the shore.

Packet boat—A small ship, powered by either sail or steam and carrying passengers and cargo in the coastal trade.

Paddlewheel—A large wheel with paddles driven by a steam engine to propel a ship through the water.

Paixhan gun—A cannon invented by a French soldier which fired an explosive shell great distances.

Port—The left side of the ship.

Pounder—Preceded by a number, as in 6-pounder. It describes a cannon firing a projectile of a specified weight.

Prize crew—A crew put aboard a captured ship.

Quarterdeck—The stern area of a ship's upper deck set aside by the captain for official use and from which command is exercised. Used as a platform to address a crew.

Rigging—Lines, spars, shrouds, and yards used in setting sails.

Schooner—A ship with fore and aft sails, usually having two masts in which the mainmast is behind the shorter foremast.

Glossary of Nautical Terms

Shoal—A shallow-water area or a sandbar close to the surface.

Shroud—A rope giving lateral support to a mast.

Spar—A wooden pole used to support sails or rigging.

Splice the main brace—Sailor slang for drinking copious amounts of alcoholic beverages.

Square rigged—A sailing ship rig in which square cut sails are extended on yards attached to the mast horizontally. Not as maneuverable as a fore-and-aft rig but designed to sail downwind efficiently when following the trade wind routes.

Starboard—The right side of the ship.

Stay—A rope giving fore and aft support to a mast.

Storm jib—A small jib sail used in bad weather.

Struck the colors—Hauled down the ship's flags from the masthead. A sign of surrender.

Tacking ship—To beat to windward on a zigzag route so that the wind is put first on one side of the ship and then on the other.

Taffrail—The rail around the stern of the ship.

Topgallant—A square-rigged sail either at the top or close to the top of a mast.

Topsail schooner—A schooner with a square sail rigged at the top of the mainmast.

Wear ship—To turn away from the wind and put the ship on another tack.

Weatherly—A ship capable of sailing close to the wind with little leeway.

Weather gauge—To be upwind of another vessel. The best position for sailing ships in an attack on an enemy.

Weather side—The side of the ship closest to the wind.

Yard—A spar to which a sail is attached.

Index

A

Adams, President John Quincy, 119
Adventure, 94, 97
Aguila, 177, 191
Alacranes Islands, 97-98, 149, 218
Alamo, 46
Allen, Captain John M., 43, 219
Allen, Isaac, 188
Allen, Midshipman William A., 152
Ampudia, General Pedro de, 198, 200, 216
Anahuac, 4, 18, 21, 26
Ana Maria, 25, 131
Anaya, General, 136-137
Apaches, 38, 44, 180
Aransas Pass, 36, 158
Arcas Islands, 126, 131-132, 137-138
Archer, 112, 117, 222
Arista, General Mariano, 121, 128
Austin, Stephen F., 8, 19, illustration 20, 31, 36
Austin, 111, illustration 112, 117, 121, 123, 128, 138, 160, 193, 196-197, 200, 204, 211-212, 222, 225

B

Baker, Captain Moseley, 53
Barrington, William, 151, 153, 188, 190, 209
Baudin, Admiral Charles, 109
Bolivar Peninsula, 51
Bollaert, William, 27, sketch by 113, 156-159
Boylan, Captain James D., 89-90, 92-93, 97-99, 101-102, 105, 125, 192, 195, 212, 230
Bradburn, Colonel John Davis, 7, 11, 14, 18, 59
Branch T. Archer, 101-102
Bravo, General Nicolas, 81
Bravo, 40, 62
Brazoria, 3, 12-13, 21, 45
Brazosport, 27, 142
Brazos River, 30, 55, 73
Brazos Santiago, 76
Brown, George, 62, 230
Brown, Captain Jeremiah, 6, 61-63, 66, 86
Brown, Captain William S., 48-49, 62, 230
Brutus, 48, illustration 51, 64, 72, 85, 88, 96-97, 103
Bryan, William, 181-182, 184
Bryant, Midshipman Andrew J., 209
Burnet, David G., 53, 145

Index

Burton, Major Isaac, 58-59

C

Campechano, 177, 191
Campeche, 69-70, 126-127, 133, 165, 186, 197, 198, 200-202, 204, 212, 229
Canon, 6
Carmen, 162-163, 165
Champion, 82-84
Charlewood, Captain E.P., 192
Chiapas, 108
Chilbona, 92
Chiltepec, 99
Cleveland, Captain Richard, 197
Climax, 83
Comanche, 60, 67
Comanches, 38, 44, 121, 143, 180
Conchita, 130
Cooke, Lewis P., 138
Copano, 36, 45, 58-60
Correo de Campeche, 43, 71
Correo de Mexico, 25-26, 39, 104-105
Correo Segundo, 62
Correo de Tabasco, 68, 98, 99
Cos, General Martin Perfecto, 36, 43
Crockett, David, 46
Cox, Midshipman Cornelius, 116, 124-126, 128, 134-135, 139, 230
Cozumel, 91-92
Culp, Midshipman Fielding R., 167-168
Cummings, Lieutenant Cyrus, 163-164

D

Davis, Captain D.F.R., 73, 75-76
Dearborn, Monroe H., 151
Desert of Dead Horses, 37
Diario del Gobierno, 72
Dueling Oaks, 167-168
Durango, 50

E

Eliza Russell, 98, 104
Elliott, Captain Charles, 174

F

Fannin, Colonel James Walker, 41-42, 47
Fanny Butler, 60, 67
Father Muldoon, 78-79
Faysoux, Midshipman C.L. 168-169
Filisola, General Vicente, 44-45, 55, illustration 57, 58
Fisher, George, 4, illustration 5-6
Fisher, Samuel Rhoads, 8, 40, 42, 86, illustration 87, 88-89, 92, 103-104, 186, 230
Flash, 52, 55
Fuller, Lieutenant Charles F., 150, 188
Fuller, Midshipman George F., 168, 189-190, 192-193, 200, 206-207, 210-211, 230

Index

G

Galveston, 3, 6, 18, 21, 27, illustration 28-29, 43, 47, 50, 55, 140, 142, 186, 216, 219, 222
Galveston Coast Guards, 157, 159
Galveston Fusiliers, 157-158
Galveston Telegraph and Register, 70
General Bravo, 85, 99
General Teran, 83-85, 99
General Urrea, 82-85
Goliad, 47, 155
Gonzales, 37
Gray, Lieutenant Alfred G., 147-148, 189, 194, 196, 215
Gray, Midshipman Fairfax, 193
Great Britain, 139
Guadalupe, 176, 191-192, 197, 204, 207, 213
Gulf of Mexico, map 2, 37, 61, 81, 86, 139, 218, 228, 230

H

Hannah Elizabeth, 40
Hawkins, Charles E., 48
Harrisburg, 53, 107
Hill, Jim Dan, 139
HMS *Penguin*, 127
Horse Marines, 60
Houston, Sam, vii, 45, 47, 50, 53-55, 68, 77, 79, 86, 88, 103-104, 117-119, 140, 146, 155-156, 159-160, 165-166, 169-172, 174, 178-180, 182-184, illustration 185, 199, 215, 217, 220-221, 223-227
Hoyt, Captain Nathaniel, 69-71, 230
Hurd, Captain William A., 32-34, 39-42, 64-65, 67, 86, 230
Hudgins, James, 188

I

Iman, 177, 191
Independence, 48, 52, 72, 74-75, illustration 76, 99, 103
Independencia, Yucatan schooner, 192
Invincible, 48, 50, 64-66, 68-69, 72, 85, 88, 96-97, 100, 102-103
Isla Mujeres, 90
Iturbide, 99

J

Jack, Pat, 10, 14, 16
Jack, William, 10
Jackson, President Andrew, 119
Johns, Midshipman Edward, 162
Johnson, Colonel F.W., 16
Jones, Captain Ezekiel, 23-25
Josefa, 25
Julius Caesar, 83-84

K

Karankaws, 158
Keener, Edward, 188
Kickapoos, 180

Index

King Louis Philippe, 108
Kiowas, 38, 44, 180
Kokernot, Captain David L., 17-18, 230

L

Lafitte, 157
Laguna, 161
Laguna de Terminos, 141, 162
Lamar, Mirabeau B., 104, 110, illustration 111, 114, 121-122, 125, 143, 145
Landois, Corporal Antonio, 152-153, 188
Laura, 31
Lemus, General Pedro, 130, 133
Letters of Marque and Reprisal, 38
Leving, Lieutenant William H., 62, 64
Lewis, Lieutenant Armstrong J., 124, 141-142
Lewis, Ira R., 39
Libertador, 73-75, 99
Liberty, 42, 48, 50, 68, 72, 103
Lobos Island, 129
Lopez, Commodore Don Francisco, 76, 197
Lothrop, Commander John, 133-135, 196, 206, 222, 230
Louisiana, 82, 85

M

Mabry, Midshipman James L., 130, 230
Mahan, Admiral Alfred T., 37
Marin, Commodore Don Tomas, 202-203, 213
Martha, 22-23
Matagorda, 6, 40, 45, 50, 156
Matamoros, 23, 36, 47, 62, 69, 72, 77, 89
Matilda, 43
Mendez, Governor Santiago, 126, 149, 200-201, 218
Merida, 146, 148, 181
Mervine, Commander William, 82-84
Mexia, Jose Antonio, 48
Middleton, Midshipman Peyton, 168-169
Moctezuma, sailing schooner, 21-22, 25
Moctezuma, steamship, 176, 191-192, 197, 204, 207, 213
Monclova, 37
Moore, Edwin Ward, 110, 113, 117, 120, 128, 130, 133, 138, 142-144, 146, 148, 163, 164, 167, 169, 170, 177, 179-180, 182-184, 186-188, 191, 193-194, 196, 198, 200, 202-203, 206, 211, 214, 216-218, 220-221, 223, 225, 227-228, illustration 229, 230
Morgan, Colonel James, 69, 181, 184, 186-187, 193, 198-200, 205, 214, 216-218, 220-221, 230

Index

N
Nacogdoches, 18, 53
Nash, C.S., 124
New Orleans, 3, 6, 28, 34, 43, 50, 66, 114, 145, 150
New Orleans Bee, 66
New Orleans Commercial Bulletin, 67
New Orleans Courier, 34
New Orleans Tropic, 183, 197
New York Harbor, 68
Nueces River, 54

O
Ocampo, Lieutenant Carlos, 34, 65
Odell, Midshipman Theodore, 152
Ocean, 67
Ohio, 22
Olmecs, 136
Orleans, 77-78
O'Shaunessy, Lieutenant James S., 141
Oswald, Sergeant Seymour, 152-153, 188

P
Padre Island, 26
Paixhans, Henri Joseph, 116
Parian, 108
Paso Cavallo, 40
Pastry War, 109
Pelicano, 49-50, 228
Pelicana Mexicana, 43
Peña, José Enrique de la, 54
Peraza, Colonel Martin, 181
Piedras, Colonel José de las, 17-18

Plan de Cuernavaca, 21
Pocket, 63-66
Polk, President James, 222
Pompilly, Private Benjamin, 188
Porter, D.D., 48
Potter, Robert, 39
Presidio del Rio Grande, 173
Progreso, 160

Q
Quintana Roo, 165

R
Rafaelia, 99-100
Randolph, Lieutenant, 42-43
Red River, 16
Red Rovers, 159
Regenerador, 177
Roo, Andres Quintana, 146-148
Roosevelt, Brigadier General Theodore, Jr., vii
Rosario, 185-186
Rowan, Thomas, 161, 188
Runaway Scrape, 47, 52, 156
Rusk, General Thomas Jefferson, 58

S
Sabine, 6
Sam Houston, 100
San Antonio, 21, 37, 43-44, 156, 165, 173-174
San Antonio, 112, 117, 130, 140, 142, 145, 149-151, illustration 154, 170

Index

San Bernard, 112, 117, 123, 131, 133, 140-141, 160, 170, 222
San Felipe, 36
San Felipe, 32-33, 37, 39
San Jacinto, 47, 52, 228
San Jacinto, 112, 117, 121, 123, 132-133, 137
San Juan Bautista, 136, 139
San Juan de Ulloa, 109
San Luis Pass, 50
Santa Anna, General Antonio Lopez de, 17-19, 31, 38-39, 44-45, 47, 54-55, illustration 56, 61, 107, 109-110, 155, 159, 186, 214, 217
Santa Fe, 143-144
Sawyer, S.O., 124
Seeger, Lieutenant William, 149-150, 153, 161, 170
Segunda Fama, 129
Shepherd, Fredrick, 153, 161, 188, 209
Simpson, Corporal William, 188
Sisal, 43, 49, 69, 125, 145
Siselano, 192
Snow, Lieutenant C.B., 220, 222
Stephen F. Austin, 16
Swartwout, Samuel, 68, 183-184, 216-217

T
Tabasco, 108, 139
Tampico, 48, 69, 129
Taylor, Lieutenant John W., 73-74, 80

Tejanos, 3
Telchac, 190, 212, 215
Telegrafo, 94, 97
Tennison, Lieutenant William A., 69, 160
Terrible, 42-43
Texas coastline, 26
Texas Congress, 80, 106, 169, 178, 227
Texas Gulf Coast, 19
Texians, 3
Thomas Toby, 69-72
Thompson, Captain Henry L., 87-91, 93-96, 98, 100-101, 105, 230
Thompson, Thomas M. "Mexico," 26, 30-34, 63-64, 79-80
Tod, John G., 140
Tornel, General Don Jose Maria, 81
Travis, William Barret, 9-11, 14, 16, 21, 45, illustration 46
Treat, James, 122, 125, 127-128, 131
Treaty of Amity and Commerce, 82
Tremont, 30-31
Trinity River, 10, 16
Twin Sisters, 52
Tyler, President John, 222

U
Union, 68, 92, 97
Underhill, Midshipman Charles B., 132
Urrea, General Don Jose, 47, 58

USS *Boston*, 43
USS *Ingham*, 22-25
USS *Jackson*, 153
USS *Natchez*, 82-84
USS *Warren*, 66

V

Valera, Lieutenant Colonel Ramon, 155
Van Buren, President Martin, 119
Vasquez, General Rafael, 155-156, 165, 175
Velasco, 3, 12, 18, 27, 59-60
Vencendor del Alamo, 67-68, 74-75
Veracruz, 108-109
Villahermosa, 136

W

Walke, Midshipman Alfred, 137-138, 191, 193-196, 202, 205, 207-209, 230
Waller, Edwin, 6
Watchman, 58-59, 67
Water Witch, 16
Webb, James, 142
Wharton, John Austin, 77-79
Wharton, William Harris, 72, 77-78, 103

Wharton, 112, 117, 157, 187, 193, 197, 200, 204, 213, illustration 219, 222
Wheelwright, Captain George W., 72-73, 75, 79-80, 86, 230
White, Midshipman George W., 167-168
William Robbins, 39, 41-42
Williamson, Robert M. "Three Legged Willie," 14, illustration 15, 18
Williamson, Lieutenant William S., 131-132
Woll, General Adrian, 161, 172-173

Y

Yucatan, 49, 72, 89, 108, 121, 144, 147, 165-166, 228
Yucateo, 177, 191

Z

Zavala, Lorenzo de, 32, 110
Zavala, 110, 117, 120, 123, 126, 131, 134-135, 140, 146, 166, 170, illustration 171